COMPLEM[ENTARY]
HEALTH
Natural ways to beat stre[ss]

Edited by
Lisa Foster

The Complementary Health Guide   Third edition
Copyright ©1994
Edited by Lisa Foster
Published by English Countryside Publications
Market Link House,
Elsenham, Bishops Stortford
Herts CM22 6DY
Tel: 0279 647555

All rights reserved. No part of this book may be reproduced, stored in a retrieval system
or transmitted in any form or by any means electronic, electrostatic, magnetic tape,
mechanical, photocopying, recording or otherwise without permission
in writing from the publishers.
Although every care is taken to ensure that all information in this guide is correct at time
of going to press and all advertisers are of good standing,
inclusion in this guide does not imply any endorsement of any product
or any therapy.
The publishers accept no responsibility for any statement, error or omission.

Printed by The Magazine Printing Company, Enfield, Middlesex

ISBN 1 870112 22 9

CONTENTS

Foreword
6

Using the Guide
9

Ailments Index
10

Therapies
15

A Healthier Way of Living
67

Courses
69

Health Centres
75

Health Retreats
76

Geographical Index
78

CONFIDENCE IN COMPLEMENTARY HEALTH GROWS

By Michael Endacott

For qualified practitioners of complementary medicine, the past year has been one of significant progress. More enquiries, more patients and more treatments are being referred than ever before. Much of this interest is generated by the media and the constant flow of articles which highlight the complementary approach to some chronic condition is certain to bring enquiries.

Everyone at the Institute for Complementary Medicine feels privileged to receive requests for help and each one is given careful consideration. The enquiries range from the anguished person who is genuinely desperate for help and has been frustrated to find that, so far, no orthodox treatment has worked. The other extreme is the person who has a minor physical problem but will not take the trouble to travel to visit a qualified practitioner. These people expect a comprehensive discussion on the telephone and usually demand a home visit.

Sadly, we cannot make a diagnosis on the telephone or in a letter but we can direct the caller to an experienced practitioner who should be able to answer questions before any commitment to treatment is entered into. This is the agreement the ICM has with practitioners on the British Register of Complementary Practitioners because both patients and clients are taking the first steps to find out for themselves the range and scope of any proposed treatments. If nothing else, this initial communication serves to begin to build a sense of confidence in the practitioner.

For any treatment to be successful in the long term, the patient or client needs to play their part in changing any aspects of their lifestyle which were unhelpful, and replacing them with more positive and productive attitudes. It can be a long process, but once the healing begins, it becomes most rewarding and satisfying.

The current interest in complementary medicine is reflected in the research projects which are under way. Members of the British Register are playing their part in developing an understanding on how best to use these methods in association with conventional health care.

Osteopathy is scheduled to be examined in 1994 and the effectiveness of this treatment for low back pain compared against physiotherapy and bed rest with analgesics.

Reflexology has already been successfully used as a post operative stimulant to speed the healing process. The patients appeared to recover faster when reflexology was given but this will have to be confirmed with a bigger trial.

Aromatherapy is well known as a relaxant and it is now being used by the nursing profession as part of the general care available on wards. A module of aromatherapy, hypnotherapy and massage is now available as part of the degree in nursing accredited by Manchester University. A simplified form of hypnotherapy is used as a means of stress control for patients on the wards.

Homoeopathy is being used to assess what help can be given to ME sufferers. For some doctors, this difficult problem is not even considered an identifiable illness. However, this coming year may well see some progress towards a better understanding of the problem.

Counselling and psychotherapy continue to be well used although the public is careful to check out the qualifications of practitioners before having treatment. Considerable anxiety about the use of trance and loss of personal contact continues to be the major worry for clients wishing to used hypnotherapy. A recent television series showing people apparently acting under the control of a hypnotist and losing their own self control has been considered entertainment. However, we do not agree and it should be pointed out that no professional hypnotherapist would seek to 'control' the patient as part of a treatment. The numbers of those who can be entranced to the depth required for this work is very small and probably accounts for less than about two per cent of the population.

Complementary Medicine is generally very safe in qualified hands and this accounts for the increasing numbers of patients who wish to check the credentials of practitioners. They need to have an assurance that they will be treated safely, correctly and ethically guided through a programme of treatment. Since these treatments are not usually available on the NHS, they can prove expensive. This is why we suggest that everyone checks a number of points before agreeing to a course of treatment.

1) Note the letters after the practitioner's name and check that this is a formal qualification. Some letters simply mean membership of an interest group and do not indicate proficiency.

2) Check that the practitioner is insured and subject to a code of conduct and practice. This will follow from question one.

3) Ask if the practitioner thinks that your condition can be helped by the treatment and find out the success rate for similar cases.

4) Ask how many treatments are likely to be needed and how much they will cost.

When you have satisfied yourself on these points, you will have a base on which to begin. Please remember that in complementary medicine you will play a part in your treatments and you will form a partnership with your practitioner. You should feel able to converse easily and know that your case is receiving undivided attention. There may well be times when the symptoms appear to get worse but this is often to be expected and is called a 'healing crisis'. However, if pain is markedly increased after any structural treatment such as chiropractic or osteopathy and you were not warned about this beforehand, contact your practitioner immediately.

Health is precious and we usually take it for granted. Problems usually take many weeks, even months, to develop and we need to realise that all healing takes time. For many, the complementary practitioner can help to bring relief of symptoms quite quickly, but for others it may be a long job. This is where a quiet determination to get well can be allied to a reflective appreciation on how to remove unhelpful elements of the lifestyle. Of equal importance is the coming to terms with aspects which cannot be changed and here an attitude of acceptance is helpful.

The future of complementary medicine looks bright but it can only continue to gain acceptance if research and qualifications follow the established routes to accreditation. Much development work is currently going on to create National Vocational Qualifications for all the therapies and this will add to the safety measures already designed to protect the general public.

It is a sad fact that many practitioners may still take short courses which are not adequate for anything more than a general relaxation treatment and yet are allowed to describe themselves as a therapist/practitioner. Some insurance policies do not allow the therapist to treat any illness. Since the therapist may not have been taught how to recognise illness, the public may be at risk.

In spite of all these problems, the number of formal complaints is few and the British Register has only received one complaint this year. The public is becoming cautious but successful treatments and competent practitioners receive recommendations by word of mouth. In the same way, incompetence and poor practice receive similar publicity and this is the main reason why so many therapists go out of business.

The publishers of this guide can only present information supplied by the advertisers. They do not have reference to any national qualification or any umbrella listing because these do not yet exist. The best that can be done is to suggest that readers check with the Institute for Complementary Medicine, PO Box 194, London SE16 1QZ. Tel: 071 237 5165. Please send an SAE, three loose stamps and state the nature of the enquiry. The ICM deals with facts not opinions and if you require information on practitioners, please include details of any letters which are printed after their name.

Complementary medicine can help so many different conditions that it is impossible to offer specific guidance. However, it is wise to ensure that you receive a diagnosis from your GP and that you tell him you are going to a complementary practitioner. If you are on any form of drug it is important that your doctor can monitor any change in your condition. Under no circumstances give up taking drugs without telling your doctor.

Taking a greater interest in your own health and playing a part in your own healing can bring about many helpful changes. I hope this guide may be the first step towards renewed health for you.

Michael Endacott is Research Director of
The Institute for Complementary Medicine

USING THIS GUIDE

This guide is designed for those who are new to complementary medicine, who may find a therapy to ease a long standing complaint in these pages and for those who understand the principles of holistic medicine and want to find out more about a particular therapy.

The emphasis of all natural medicine is the maintenance of health rather than the treatment of disease. Good car maintenance does not consist of waiting until the car breaks down and then trying to find a fix! This is the primary difference between conventional and complementary medicine. The therapeutic techniques described here are designed to maintain health and create well-being as well as to ease specific ailments.

If you are looking for a specific therapy, the alphabetical listings of therapies will guide you to it. If you have a problem that you think might be helped by complementary medicine, the index on page 11 lists some common ailments and suggests therapies which might be appropriate. This can only be a very rough starting point, though, as the whole concept of complementary medicine is to look at the patient as a whole and find the appropriate cure for that person, rather than to use the conventional system of always treating the same symptom with the same remedy.

At the back of the book is a selection of courses for those who want to take their knowledge of complementary medicine further and a list of the professional associations and regulatory bodies concerned with complementary health in the United Kingdom. All will be able to advise on qualified practitioners in your locality.

Lisa Foster
Editor

A HARMONY OF SCIENCE AND NATURE

STOP! BEFORE YOU BUY

JUICERS, WATER PURIFIERS, AIR IONISERS, AEROBIC BOUNCERS, ENEMA KITS, GRAIN MILLS, BACK SWINGS, SLANT-BOARDS, IRIDOLOGY & NATURAL FERTILITY AWARENESS EQUIPMENT, MAGNETIC FOIL, BIO-CRYSTAL PULSORS, HERBAL TABLET MAKERS, DOWSING RODS, HUMANE MOUSE TRAPS, REFLEX FOOT ROLLERS, ALOE VERA PLANTS, S/S STEAMERS, SUNBOXES, DAYLIGHT SPECTRUM LIGHTING, VDU FILTERS, ALLERGY CONTROL EQUIPMENT & LOADS OF BOOKS ON THESE AND OTHER HEALTH TOPICS.

GET ALL THE FACTS

from our famous 72 page book:

A HARMONY OF SCIENCE AND NATURE
Ways of Staying Healthy in a Modern World
by John & Lucie Davidson

It's full of background information, plus full product details.
Send £1.00 (or 6x2nd CLASS STAMPS)!
Limited period only - sold in bookshop for £3.95.
It's essential reading - everyone should have a copy.

OVER 300 SELECTED PRODUCTS AND BOOKS

WHOLISTIC RESEARCH COMPANY
Dept. CH, Bright Haven, Robin's Lane, Lolworth,
Cambridge CB3 8HH
Telephone: Craft's Hill (0945) 781074 (24 hrs)
Agent & Trade enquiries welcome

BOOK OFFER!

AILMENTS INDEX

There are no hard and fast rules to symptoms and cures in complementary medicine as the principle is to look at the whole body rather than individual ailments. Two people suffering the same symptoms may need totally different treatments. The orthodox cure for a headache might be an aspirin whatever the cause of the headache, but a holistic practitioner will aim to find the root cause of a headache and aim to correct it there.

But newcomers to this very different concept in medicine do need a guide to where to start seeking help and this ailments index makes a variety of suggestions for suitable therapies. It is by no means comprehensive and does not include therapies which might alleviate some of the symptoms of serious mental or physical illness although they cannot offer a cure. For example cancer patients can find megavitamin therapy beneficial and yoga, herbal medicine, aromatherapy and homoeopathy can all help in the treatment of diabetes, but such treatments and therapies need to be worked out with the close co-operation of the patient, orthodox practitioners and complementary therapists.

ABDOMINAL PROBLEMS
Colonic hydrotherapy
Dietary therapeutics
Homoeopathy
Iridology
Kinesiology

ADDICTION
Art therapy
Chinese medicine
Counselling
Dance movement therapy
Floatation therapy
Hypnotherapy
Integral psychoanalysis
Megavitamin therapy
Neuro-linguistic programming
Psychotherapy

ALLERGIES
Acupressure
Acupuncture
Allergy therapy
Chinese medicine
Dietary therapeutics
Herbal medicine
Homoeopathy
Integral psychoanalysis
Kinesiology

ANAEMIA
Aromatherapy
Herbal medicine
Homoeopathy
Chinese medicine

ANXIETY
Acupuncture
Autogenic training
Chinese medicine
Counselling
Dance movement therapy
Floatation therapy
Homoeopathy
Hypnotherapy
Massage
Meditation
Metamorphic technique
Neuro-linguistic programming
Polarity therapy
Psychotherapy

ANXIETY (CONT)
Rebirthing
Regression therapy
Reiki
Rolfing
Shiatsu
Stress management
Tape Yoga

APATHY/ LISTLESSNESS
Homoeopathy
Metamorphic technique
Nutritional therapy
Polarity therapy
Rebirthing
Radiance Technique
Regression therapy

ARTHRITIS
Acupressure
Acupuncture
Alexander Technique
Aromatherapy
Chinese medicine
Dietary therapeutics
Feldenkrais Method
Herbal medicine
Homoeopathy
Mesotherapy
Osteopathy
Ozone therapy
Polarity therapy
Reiki
Rolfing
Yoga

ASTHMA
Acupressure
Acupuncture
Alexander Technique
Allergy therapy
Biofeedback
Chinese medicine
Colour therapy
Cranio sacral therapy
Homoeopathy
Hypnotherapy
Kinesiology
Polarity therapy
Yoga

BACK PROBLEMS	Acupressure Acupuncture Alexander Technique Aromatherapy Biofeedback Chinese medicine Chiropractic Cranio sacral therapy Feldenkrais Method Hellerwork Kinesiology Mesotherapy Muscle learning therapy Osteopathy Polarity therapy Reflexology Rolfing Shiatsu	**DIGESTIVE PROBLEMS**	Acupressure Acupuncture Aromatherapy Chinese medicine Colonic hydrotherapy Colour therapy Cranio sacral therapy Dietary therapeutics Homoeopathy Iridology Kinesiology Polarity therapy Reflexology Shiatsu
CIRCULATION PROBLEMS	Acupressure Aromatherapy Chelation therapy Chinese medicine Massage Meditation Mesotherapy Ozone therapy Polarity therapy Reflexology Shiatsu	**EATING DISORDERS**	Art therapy Colonic hydrotherapy Dance movement therapy Polarity therapy Psychotherapy
		ECZEMA	Allergy therapy Aromatherapy Colour therapy Dietary therapeutics Herbal medicine Homoeopathy Hypnotherapy Kinesiology Ozone therapy
CONSTIPATION	Aromatherapy Colonic hydrotherapy Cranio sacral therapy Homoeopathy Muscle learning therapy Polarity therapy Reflexology Shiatsu	**EMOTIONAL PROBLEMS**	Art therapy Colour therapy Counselling Cranio sacral therapy Metamorphic technique Neuro-linguistic programming Psychotherapy Radiance Technique Rolfing Shiatsu
DEPRESSION	Acupressure Alexander Technique Aromatherapy Autogenic training Counselling Colour therapy Cranio sacral therapy Dance movement therapy Dietary therapeutics Integral psychoanalysis Kinesiology Megavitamin therapy Metamorphic technique Neuro-linguistic programming Nutritional therapy Polarity therapy Psychotherapy Radiance Technique Rebirthing Reflexology Reiki Rolfing	**EYE STRAIN**	The Bates Method Indian head massage (see Massage)
		FATIGUE	Acupressure Acupuncture Alexander Technique Cranio sacral therapy Hellerwork Homoeopathy Kinesiology Nutritional therapy Radiance Technique Regression therapy Reiki Rolfing Shiatsu
		FLUID RETENTION	Aromatherapy Mesotherapy Polarity therapy
		FUNGAL INFECTIONS	Aromatherapy Colonic hydrotherapy Ozone therapy

HAY FEVER	Allergy therapy Dietary therapeutics Homoeopathy	**IRRITABLE BOWEL SYNDROME**	Alexander Technique Autogenic training Biofeedback Herbal medicine
HEADACHES	Acupressure Alexander Technique Aromatherapy Biofeedback Chinese medicine Chiropractic Colonic hydrotherapy Cranio sacral therapy Hellerwork Herbal medicine Homoeopathy Integral psychoanalysis Indian head massage (see Massage) Iridology Kinesiology Meditation Muscle learning therapy Osteopathy Polarity therapy Reflexology Reiki Shiatsu Yoga	**LEG ULCERS**	Chelation therapy Dietary therapeutics Homoeopathy Mesotherapy Ozone therapy
		MENTAL PROBLEMS	Art therapy Counselling Dance movement therapy Integral psychoanalysis Music, sound and voice Psychotherapy Reflexology Shiatsu
		MIGRAINE	Acupressure Aromatherapy Autogenic training Biofeedback Chinese medicine Colour therapy Cranio sacral therapy Herbal medicine Homoeopathy Hypnotherapy Indian head massage (see Massage) Integral psychoanalysis Mesotherapy Reflexology Shiatsu
HEART PROBLEMS	Acupuncture Chelation therapy Dietary therapeutics Ozone therapy Reflexology		
HIGH BLOOD PRESSURE	Autogenic training Biofeedback Chelation therapy Colour therapy Dietary therapeutics Floatation therapy Iridology Massage Meditation Polarity therapy Rebirthing		
		MUSCULAR TENSION	Acupressure Alexander Technique Aromatherapy Autogenic training Biofeedback Chiropractic Hellerwork Kinesiology Massage Meditation Mesotherapy Muscle learning therapy Osteopathy Polarity therapy Rolfing Shiatsu
INCONTINENCE	Muscle learning therapy		
INDIGESTION	Acupressure Acupuncture Autogenic training Herbal medicine		
INSOMNIA	Acupressure Acupuncture Aromatherapy Autogenic training Cranio sacral therapy Floatation therapy Homoeopathy Hypnotherapy Indian head massage (see Massage) Meditation Reflexology Shiatsu	**NEUROSIS**	Art therapy Counselling Dance movement therapy Hypnotherapy Metamorphic technique Neuro-linguistic programming Polarity therapy Psychotherapy

NEURO-MUSCULAR DIFFICULTIES	Feldenkrais Method	**RESPIRATORY DISORDERS**	Acupuncture Alexander Technique Autogenic training Cranio sacral therapy Homoeopathy Polarity therapy
PAIN RELIEF	Acupressure Acupuncture Alexander Technique Aromatherapy Autogenic training Biofeedback Chiropractic Colour therapy Cranio sacral therapy Feldenkrais Method Hellerwork Homoeopathy Kinesiology Massage Meditation Mesotherapy Muscle learning therapy Osteopathy Polarity therapy Reflexology Reiki Shiatsu Spiritual healing	**SKIN DISORDERS**	Acupuncture Allergy therapy Chinese medicine Hypnotherapy Nutritional therapy Ozone therapy
		SPINAL DISORDERS	Chiropractic Feldenkrais Method Hellerwork Herbal medicine Homoeopathy Osteopathy Rolfing
		SPORTS INJURIES	Acupuncture Chiropractic Mesotherapy Osteopathy
PHOBIAS	Homoeopathy Hypnotherapy Integral psychoanalysis Kinesiology Neuro-linguistic programming Psychotherapy	**STRESS**	Acupressure Acupuncture Alexander Technique Aromatherapy Autogenic training Colour therapy Counselling Crystal healing Dance movement therapy Feldenkrais Method Floatation therapy Hellerwork Hypnotherapy Integral psychoanalysis Kinesiology Massage Meditation Metamorphic technique Polarity therapy Psychotherapy Radiance Technique Rebirthing Reflexology Reiki Shiatsu Stress management Tape relaxation Yoga
POOR CONCENTRATION	Alexander Technique Meditation Nutritional therapy Radiance Technique		
POOR VISION	The Bates Method		
POSTURE	Alexander Technique Aston Patterning Cranio sacral therapy Hellerwork Muscle learning therapy Osteopathy Polarity therapy Rolfing Yoga		
PREGNANCY PROBLEMS	Chiropractic Osteopathy Rebirthing		
		ULCERS	Acupuncture Autogenic training Bio Feedback Hypnotherapy Ozone therapy
PRE MENSTRUAL TENSION	Acupuncture Aromatherapy Colonic hydrotherapy Dietary therapeutics Homoeopathy Kinesiology Polarity therapy		

ACUPRESSURE

Acupressure is an ancient massage skill sometimes referred to as "acupuncture without needles". It works by stimulating the points with the help of pressure from the fingers and the thumbs.

Simple and easy, acupressure is an effective self-treatment with no side-effects. A short session in the morning helps to maintain the balance of energy flowing through the body which leads to the prevention of disease.

It helps to increase vitality and strength, alleviates stress related symptoms, stiffness, PMT, asthma, headaches, insomnia, back pain, digestion problems, poor circulation and allergies.

For further help contact:
T H Jivraj BSc DHom (Med)
D Acupressure, Cert in
Counselling,
Natural Health Clinic,
286 Preston Road, Harrow,
Middx HA3 0QA
Tel 081-908 4272

**Enrico Dodson, 21
Cowlersley Lane,
Cowlersley,
Huddersfield HP4 5TY
Tel: 0484 641982**

ACUPUNCTURE

Acupuncture is an ancient Chinese therapy and today, world-wide, there are over three million practitioners.

Acupuncture began with the discovery that the stimulation of specific areas of the skin affected the functioning of certain organs of the body. It evolved into a system of healing as the connection between the skin and the organs was better understood and more sensitive ways of stimulation were devised.

In the West, acupuncture has been misleadingly publicised as only being helpful in specific conditions, for example, pain or weight loss; whereas, in fact, it is extremely effective in a wide variety of conditions through its power to stimulate our own healing responses. This overall therapeutic effect is one of its greatest strengths.

Patients are treated by sticking needles into their skin at particular points. These acupuncture points lie along invisible energy channels called "meridians" which are believed to be linked to internal organs. The needles are said to unblock, increase or decrease a flow of energy through the meridians.

Acupuncture has been found to help people suffering from allergy, angina, anxiety, asthma, bronchitis, colitis, digestive problems, gall-bladder problems, insomnia, stress, tiredness and ulcers. Success has been claimed in relieving withdrawal symptoms after giving up smoking and other types of addiction.

In general, acupuncture works in stages and improvement should build up in successive sessions. However, if there is no improvement after six to eight sessions, acupuncture is unlikely to work. Many traditional acupuncturists recommend three or four visits a year.

For further help contact:
British Acupuncture
Association and Register
34 Alderney Street
London SW1V 4EU
Tel: 071-834 1012

British College of Acupuncture
8 Hunter Street
London WC1N 1BN
Tel 071-833 8164

Council for Acupuncture
179 Gloucester Place
London NW1 6DX
Tel 071-724 5756

Complementary Medicine
Centre, 9 Corporation Street,
Taunton, Somerset TA1 4AJ
Tel: 0823 325022

The Notting Hill Traditional
Acupuncture Centre,
21 Ladbroke Grove, London
W11 3AY.
Tel: 071 221 1326

Fook Song Acupuncture and
Chinese Herbal Practitioners
Training College
1037B Finchley Road,
Golders Green
London NW11 7ES
Tel: 081 455 5508

**Heather Algar BA Lic Ac
Member of The Traditional
Acupuncture Society.
ACUPUNCTURE combined
with therapeutic massage,
giving effective treatment for
many stress related
problems. Tel: (Hampstead)
071 483 2156**

Acu Medic Centre
101-103 Camden High Street,
London NW1 7JN
Tel: 071 388 5783/388 6704
Fax: 071 387 5766
Telex: 269460 ACUMED G

H Simpson, DO NCSO,
MGO(Lon), MICAK, MRSH,
MHPA, MAA, MCKORE
Merseyside Tel: 0744 883737

Martin Harvey BA MRTCM
Natural Choice Therapy C'ntre
24 St John Street, Ashbourne,
Derbyshire DE6 1GH
Tel: 0335 346096S

Natural Healing Centre
72 Pasture Road, Goole,
North Humberside DN14 6HE
Tel: 0405 769119.

The Notting Hill Traditional Acupuncture Centre,
21 Ladbroke Grove, London W11 3AY.
Tel: 071 221 1326

ACUPUNCTURE, ALEXANDER TECHNIQUE,
CHINESE HERBS, HOMOEOPATHY, IOKAI SHIATSU,
MASSAGE, OSTEOPATHY, YOGA

FOOK SANG ACUPUNTURE AND CHINESE HERBAL PRACTITIONERS TRAINING COLLEGE

A unique opportunity to acquire correct training in the traditional methods of both Chinese Acupuncture and Chinese Herbal Medicine, enabling future practice with full confidence. Membership for graduates. Courses: Weekends by Chinese Practitioners. Close links with China. Write to:
The Registrar
1037B Finchley Road, Golders Green
London NW11 7ES Tel: 081 455 5508

THE ALEXANDER TECHNIQUE

The Alexander Technique addresses the fundamental causes of many medical conditions such as back pain, neck and shoulder tension, breathing disorders, stress-related illnesses and general fatigue where postural problems and loss of poise are contributory factors.

Because it is concerned with the quality of movement, the technique can benefit anyone with the interest to pursue it. Pupils learn to appreciate the practical implications of thought on muscle activity. A teacher's hands encourage a specific

STAT

The Society of Teachers of the Alexander Technique

For further information and a list of teachers who have completed a three-year training, send a stamped addressed envelope to:

STAT
20 London House. 266 Fulham Road,
London SW10 9EL
Tel: 071 351 0828

Acu Medic CENTRE
101-103 CAMDEN HIGH STREET, LONDON NW1 7JN
TEL: 071 388 5783/388 6704 FAX: 071 387 5766
TELEX: 269460 ACUMED G

quality of muscle tone. Together with words of instruction, this helps to release inappropriate tension and allows the body to become better aligned and balanced. Apart from short introductory courses, the Alexander Technique is taught individually.

The Society of Teachers of the Alexander Technique (STAT) was established in 1958 and is the internationally recognised body with over 1,200 members worldwide and over 500 teachers in the UK. They are professionally qualified and adhere to a published code of ethics.

Affiliated societies exist in North America and Canada and in Denmark, Germany, Israel, Switzerland and South Africa.

Standards of training are monitored by the society. All its members have completed a three year, full time training course to a standard approved by the society.

For further help contact:

The Society of Teachers of the Alexander Technique
20 London House,
266 Fulham Road,
London SW10 9EL
071 351 0828

ALEXANDER TEACHING NETWORK
For a list of qualified teachers of the Alexander Technique throughout the country.
PO Box 53, Kendal, Cumbria LA9 4UP

Lynn Sullivan SRN STAT
Violet Hill Studios,
Centre for Creative Healing,
6 Violet Hill,
St John's Wood,
London NW8 9EB
Tel: 071 602 7629
Violet Hill Studios
tel: 071 624 6101

David Glassman MSTAT
26 Cleveland Gardens
London NW2 1DY
Tel: 081 455 1317
(also City practice)

Alexander Technique
Private lessons
Introductory workshops
Evening classes
STAT Qualified teachers
BLOOMSBURY
ALEXANDER CENTRE
80a Southampton Row,
London WC1B 4BB
Tel: 071 404 5348

Nicola Harris BA MSTAT
Teacher of the Alexander Technique, Natural Choice Therapy Centre 24 St John Street, Ashbourne, Derbyshire DE6 1GH
Tel: 0335 346096

Mrs Shirley Crawford MSTAT
The Old School House
Ide Hill, Sevenoaks
Kent TN14 6JT
Tel: 0732 750246

Colin Barr CH
Wolverhampton
Tel: 0902 734861

Sheila Parry MSTAT GBC teaches at the Quay Arts Centre, Newport, Isle of Wight and at Little Whitehouse, Whitehouse Cross, Porchfield.
Telephone for all appointments and information 0983 520211

Stephen Cooper
10 York Street, Headington, Oxford OX3 8NW
Tel: 0865 65511 and Bristol House
80a Southampton Row, London WC1B 4BA
Tel 071 404 5348
Also teaches Alexander Technique and is Director of Oxford Alexander Training School

ALEXANDER TECHNIQUE

- Private lessons
- Introductory Workshops & Evening Classes
- STAT Qualified Teachers

BLOOMSBURY ALEXANDER CENTRE
80a Southampton Row, London WC1B 4BB

071 404 5348

ALLERGY THERAPY

For over 2,000 years, it has been recognised that some people react badly to certain foods, dust, pollens and fumes and become ill as a result. The classic allergic response can be seen in, for instance, hay fever, uticarial rashes, asthma and eczema.

The range of illnesses which may be caused by allergy is very wide indeed - persistent tiredness, migraine and depression, for example. Many illnesses which have previously been thought to be 'all in the mind' may be successfully treated.

Food allergies can be identified and treated by avoidance diets, many other allergens by skin scratch tests or laboratory blood tests. Muscle testing and the Vega test have proved to be extremely effective.

The therapist may use muscle testing to identify the suspected allergens, then prepare a course of desensitisation treatment designed to lead to steady improvement in health. This may take the form of specially homoeopathically potentised allergens taken in the form of drops by mouth.

For further help contact:
The Institute of Allergy Therapists
Ffynnonwen, Llangwryfon,
Aberystwyth,
Dyfed SY23 4EY
Tel: 09747 376

T H Jivraj BSc DHom (Med) Cert in Counselling,
Natural Health Clinic,
286 Preston Road, Harrow,
Middx HA3 0QA
Tel O81-908 4272

Complementary Medicine Centre
9 Corporation Street, Taunton,
Somerset TA1 4AJ
Tel: 0823 325022

H Simpson, DO NCSO, MGO(Lon), MICAK, MRSH, MHPA, MAA, MCKORE Tel: 0744 883737

Allergy Relief Products Ltd
Mansion House, Mansion Rd,
Southampton SO1 3BP
Tel: 0703 332919/586709
Fax: 0703 676226

General Designs Ltd
(Pastarisa/Ener-G Foods Distributor)
PO Box 38, Kingston, Surrey
KT2 7YP
Tel: 081 336 2323

ANTHROPO-SOPHICAL MEDICINE

Anthroposophical medicine is an alternative for people who want to use drugs or surgery as little as possible.

It is practised exclusively by conventionally qualified doctors who use a wide range of medicines composed of natural substances in conjunction with artistic therapies and also hydrotherapy and massage.

Through anthroposophy - the study founded by scientist and philosopher Rudolph Steiner - it is possible to experience that the human being has a spiritual as well as mental and physical constitution. Anthoroposophical medicine supports the patient's own healing processes.

For further help contact:
Anthroposophical Medical Association
Rudolf Steiner House
35 Park Rd, London NW1 6XT

The Natural Shoe Store
21 Neal Street, London WC2
Tel: 071 836 5254
325 Kings Road, London SW3
Tel: 071 351 3721
22 Princes Square
Buchanan Street, Glasgow
Tel: 041 226 3356
Mail order: 071 602 9657

HOUSE DUST MITE – ARE YOU ALLERGIC?

Then fit a **DERPI DUSTOP** bedding cover
Details: Allergy Relief Products Ltd,
Mansion House, Mansion Road, Southampton, Hants SO1 3BP
Tel: 0703 332919/586709 Fax: 0703 676226

THE NATURAL SHOE STORE

The famous Footbed sandal

BIRKENSTOCK
A Step Ahead

Step into the original contoured footbed sandals and you step into comfort. Birkenstock sandals and shoes cup cushion and comfort every inch of the foot, while they support the arches and leave room to stretch the toes. You owe it to yourself to try Birkenstock.

Mail order Catalogue - Now available.
Ring 071 602 9657 See them at:

**21 NEAL STREET, WC2
TEL: 071 836 5254
325 KINGS ROAD, SW3
TEL: 071 351 3721
22 PRINCES SQUARE, BUCHANAN STREET, GLASGOW
TEL: 041 226 3356**

Fleur
AROMATHERAPY

introductory courses

These courses are designed for beginners wishing to learn and experience first hand how essential oils and massage can enhance their lives ● to learn simple ways of helping family and friends or those considering starting a career in Aromatherapy

pure essential oils

from verified botanical species of known origins all analysed and tested for purity

Vital Organic Essential Oils
Cold pressed carrier oils ● Bath & Massage oils
Aromatherapy starter kits ● Gift packs
Room fragrancers ● Diffusers ● Storage cases
Practitioner case

Pembroke Studios ● Pembroke Road
● London N10
Tel: 081 444 7424 Fax: 081 444 0704

DIETARY FOODS

Free from Gluten, Wheat, Soya, Maize, Lactose, Egg or Milk. No refined sugar or artificial additives

**BREADS
PASTAS
BRAN
EGG REPLACER**

pastariso

For further information contact:
**General Designs Ltd
(Pastarisa/Ener-G Foods Distributor)**
PO Box 38, Kingston, Surrey KT2 7YP
or call us on

081 336 2323

Shirley Price
AROMATHERAPY

**SHIRLEY PRICE AROMATHERAPY COLLEGE
AROMATHERAPY TRAINING COURSES**
An inter-related, fexible, modular system of training held in 11 different Uk training venues

- AROMATHERAPY FOUNDATION COURSE
- AROMATHERAPY BODYWORK CERTIFICATE COURSE including ANATOMY & PHYSIOLOGY
- SPECIAL AROMATHERAPY COURSES FOR NURSES
- POST GRADUATE COURSES
- THE CLINICAL PRACTITIONERS DIPLOMA
- THE CHEMISTRY OF ESSENTIAL OILS & CARRIER OILS

Courses approved by
The International Society of Professional Aromatherapists

For full particulars, contact:
The Shirley Price Aromatherapy College,
PO Box 29, Hinckley, Leicestershire, LE10 0FT
Tel: 0455 615466 Fax: 0455 615054

AROMA THERAPY

Aromatherapy is the art and science of using essential oils from aromatic plants for the enhancement of health and well being. It is a holistic therapy as it looks at the whole person and not only at an isolated complaint.

It is an ancient therapeutic treatment which enhances well being, relieves stress and helps in the rejuvenation and regeneration of the human body.

This method of massaging essential oils into the body using different techniques, has been used throughout history in the medical practices of the world's greatest civilisations.

Today is it recognised by orthodox practitioners as one of the most natural and beneficial alternative therapies.

It should be considered an energetic and a scientifically based therapy to be undertaken by clinically trained therapists who possess a good knowledge of all aspects of aromatic plant botany, chemistry of essential oils, consultation procedures and an understanding of the process of disease. The therapist also requires counselling skills, and the ability to receive referrals from the client's GP and to communicate with health professionals without any difficulty.

Aromatherapy has a relaxing and anti-stress effect, commonly considered as a beauty therapy massage or pampering.

Depending on their training, aromatherapists specialise either in aesthetic aromatherapy, psychoaromatherapy, or clinical aromatherapy, the latter dealing with a variety of female complaints, children's ailments, arthritis disorders and skin disorders, to name just a few areas of specialised aomatherapeutic treatments.

The main aromatherapeutic treatment involves skilful massage with an individually formulated blend of essential oils in a base carrier oil, although other recommended treatments may include inhalations, the use of compresses, aromatic baths and vaporisers.

Essential oils are a vital part of aromatheraphy. These oils are pure, aromatic essences which are extracted or distilled forms from flowers, trees, herbs and fruit. Each oil has its own unique property. Some are used for relieving stress or nervous related disorders, others stimulate and rejuvenate, certain essences aid circulation and can be used to treat many diverse conditions.

Massage is the most beneficial method of distributing the essential oils. The therapist uses his skills and knowledge of blood and lymph pressure flow, stress and release points, and relaxation points to achieve maximum results.

As the scientific underpinning of aromatherapy grows internationally, so does the need for well trained therapists who possess a working knowledge of at least 50 different essential oils with their various indications and contra-indications.

The need for continuous update is now well understood by members of the leading aromatherapy organisations such as the International Federation of Aromatherapists and the Aromatherapy Organisations Council.

You don't have to be ill to consult a therapist. Many people find sleep patterns and energy levels are improved as well as having a more relaxed mind and body. Every day aches and pains are alleviated.

For further help contact:

International Federation of Aromatherapists
IFA Department of Continuing Education, The Royal Masonic Hospital, Ravenscroft Park.
London W6 0TN
Tel: 081 846 8066

The International Society of Professional Aromatherapists
41 Leicester Road, Hinckley,
Leics LE10 1LW
Tel: 0455 637987

Institute of Traditional Herbal
Medicine and Aromatherapy
15 Coolhurst Road,
London N8 8EP
Tel: 081 348 3755

The International Academy of
Holistic Studies
PO Box 210 Romford
Essex RM7 7DW

Fleur
Pembroke Studios,
Pembroke Road. London N10
Tel: 081 444 7424
Fax: 081 444 0704

Jill Norfolk, Professionally
ITEC Qualified MISPA
Bracknell, Berkshire
Tel: 0344 302555

Aromatherapy, Holistic massage and counselling, Taichi & Yoga classes. Wide variety of courses/workshops/products. Wheelchair access throughout. Workshop/treatment space to live. **Swanfleet Centre 93 Fortress Road, London NW5 1AG Tel: 071 267 6717**

Brenda Coverdale Accredited Tutor of Aromatherapy and Reflexology 16 Sunnyhill Road, Streatham, London SW16 2UH Telephone 081 6646150

Complementary Medicine Centre, 9 Corporation Street, Taunton, Somerset TA1 4AJ
Tel: 0823 325022

Philippa Hunter – Tisserand trained and registered. Holistic Aromatherapist. Effective treatment for stress, tension and related disorders. The Old Convent, Beeches Green, Stroud, Glos
Tel: 0453 756143

Bay House Aromatics
296a Ditchling Road
Brighton BN1 6JG
Tel: 0273 559444
Fax: 0273 559444

I D Aromatics
12 New Station Street,
Leeds LS1 5FL.
Tel: 0532 424983

Dr Marsh
121 Byron Way, Northolt
Middlesex UB5 6BA
Tel/fax: 081 845 8582

International Federation of Aromatherapists

The International Federation of Aromatherapists is one of the leading and established independent professional bodies representing Aromatherapists in the UK.

Founded in 1985 by a group of the country's leading Aromatherapists, its main aims are to represent Aromatherapists and at the same time safeguard the general public by ensuring high professional standards.

Significant resources have been devoted to professional development including training offered to a high standard by IFA registered courses which are taught by IFA registered teachers. On completetion of these courses Graduates are eligible to sit the IFA's External Examinations to obtain Full Membership of the organisation.

The Aromatherapy in Care Programme was set up in 1988 and supports IFA volunteers working within the NHS, Hospices and Childrens Homes.Aromatherapists who are Full Members of the IFA have comprehensive insurance and are entitled to use the letters MIFA after their name.

The IFA publishes a Directory of Full Members and a Registered Courses Booklet. Both are updated annually and can be obtained by sending an A5 sae and a cheque for £1.50 payable to the IFA to:

IFA Department of Continuing Education,
The Royal Masonic Hospital, Ravenscroft Park. London W6 0TN
Tel: 081 846 8066

Teresa Munro
AROMATHERAPY

The Aromatherapy Shop, Unit 5, Keeley House Business Centre, 22-30 Keeley Road, Croydon CR0 1TE

Massage oils ● Bath oils ● Pure essential oils carrier oils Massage treatments ● Books ●. Couch rolls ● Couches
All your aromatherapy requirements whether you are a student therapist, requiring a treatment or just interested come along for a chat and discover the wonderful world of aromatherapy.

MAIL ORDER
Helpline Telephone No
081 686 7171 Ext 222 Fax No 081 680 5895

Holistic treatments for body, mind, spirit & emotions

Aromatherapy & Reflexology

Telephone for appointments

Bracknell (0344) 302555   **Jill Norfolk**

Professionally ITEC Qualified MISPA

NEW HORIZON AROMATICS

Finest Quality Essential Oils for the Aromatherapist at competitive prices. We have one of the largest selection of Aromatherapy oils for the therapist and for home use.
Please write or telephone for price list
Trade enquiries from therapists and heath practitioners welcome.

New Horizon Aromatics
Horizon House, Portsmouth Road
Bursledon, Southampton, Hants SO3 8EP
Tel: 0703 404445

THE SHEFFIELD COLLEGE
of aromatherapy, reflexology & body massage
PRINCIPAL CHRISTINE CLARKE
IFA, MAR, MIIR, C&G Cert of FE

for the most comprehensive courses of study available in the North

- AROMATHERAPY
- REFLEXOLOGY
- BODY MASSAGE
- ANATOMY OF PHYSIOLOGY

428A Ecclesall Road, Sheffield S11 8PX
Tel: 0742 682140

Lavender House
Aromatherapy & Shiatsu Centre

Esther Wai Lin Jeffries
MIFA MISPA CERT ED DIPLOMA SHIATSU-DO
& MEMBERS OF SHIATSU SOCIETY
30/31 Henley Street, Stratford-upon-Avon

Aromatherapy Diploma Course
Aromatherapy Diploma, registered with the International Federation of Aromatherapists.
Basic massage training
Postal and full training on anatomy and physiology
Shiatsu Workshops
Reflex Therapy Workshops

Part-time 1 year
Full training available
Please enquire
0789 204775

IFA REGISTERED AROMATHERAPY COURSE No. 91/2/00124

The Aromatherapy Shop
Aromatherapy and reflexology
Flat Lane, Kelsall, Cheshire
Telephone: 0829 751810

Institute of traditional herbal medicine and aromatherapy (est 1980)
AROMATHERAPY
MASSAGE DIPLOMA COURSE
16-weekend professional qualification courses:
50 essential oils, massage, oriental diagnosis, cranial therapy, anat & phys:
Write: ITHMA 15 Coolhurst Road, London N8 8EP
Telephone: 081 348 3755

Originals

AROMATHERAPY 100% pure, essential oils supplied by **MAIL ORDER**. Trade enquiries welcome. For details send SAE to:
Natural Therapy Centre, Wallerscote House, Winnington Lane, Northwich, Cheshire CW8 4EG
Tel: 0606 782233 Fax: 0606 784436

ID Aromatics has over 90 Essential Oils and over 90 Perfume Oils always in stock. Best quality Aromatherapy Oils and Absolutes. Joss Sticks, Incenses.
Highly competitive prices and fast efficient service.
Visit our retail outlet or enquire for Retail or Wholesale details.
Write for price list to:
12 New Station Street, Leeds LS1 5FL.
Tel: 0532 424983

id Aromatics

Alison Perrott SP Dip A,
MISPA, MISMA, MASK, MTMI,
The S.E.E.D Institute,
10 Magnolia Way, Fleet,
Hants GU13 9JZ
Tel: 0252 626448

Natural Therapy Centre,
Wallerscote House,
Winnington Lane, Northwich,
Cheshire CW8 4EG
Tel: 0606 782233
Fax: 0606 784436

Solaire Aromatherpay
Supplies, Treatments and
Tuition
Extensive selection of
essential oils and sundries
at wholesale prices. Lucas
Close, Camberley, Surrey
GU17 7JD. Tel: 0252 873334

In Scotland learn massage in
3 wk/6wk courses, details
from Edinburgh School of
Natural Therapy, 2 London
Street, EH3 6NA
Tel: 031 557 3901

Under Stress?
Relax at Body and Soul
91 Graham Street, Airdrie,
Scotland
Aromotherapy, Reflexology
and Sugaring by
Kathryn Mc Phail GSSR IPTI
For appointments tel:
0236 756610
Gift Vouchers available.

Mr Fox, 20 High Street,
Dereham, Norfolk. Trained in
Aromatherapy, Reflexology,
Massage and Healing.
Tel: 0362 691131

Teresa Munro
The Aromatherapy Shop,
Unit 5, Keeley House Business
Centre, 22-30 Keeley Road,
Croydon CR0 1TE
Helpline: 081 686 7171 ex 222
Fax : 081 680 5895

Amphora Aromatics
An extensive range of
essential oils and
aromatherapy sundries, at
wholesaler prices. Ring or
write for a price list.
36 Cotham Hill,
Bristol BS6 6LA
Tel: 0272 738310

Lavender House
Aromatherapy & Shiatsu
Centre
30/31 Henley Street,
Stratford upon Avon
Tel: 0789 204775

AROMATHERAPY WORLD

The official quarterly publication of the International Society of Professional Aromatherapists. This Society is a rapidly expanding pro-active organisation looking towards the best interest of its therapists and the public.

For more information regarding membership, the journal or lists of registered therapists, please send a SAE to 41 Leicester Road, Hinckley, Leics LE10 1LW, or telephone 0455 637987

The International Society   ISPA   of Professional Aromatherapists

HOLISTIC APPROACH
Essential oils may be used on many levels - physical, emotional, mental and spiritual - and are ideal when used in combination with other therapies.
KOBASHI - discover for yourself the therapeutic qualities of these PURE ESSENTIAL OILS
Select from our carefully chosen range

● aromatherapy
● bathing
● hair & skin
● massage
● pottery burners - light rings

● Base products specially formulated to be used with Kobashi essential oils
● All our essential oils, pure and undiluted are from named botanical species

KOBASHI
50 High St, Ide, Exeter, Devon EX2 9RW Tel: 0392 217968
Please enclose an SAE for free Aromatherapy chart & information. Products avialable at independent health & wholefood outlets

New Horizon Aromatics
Horizon House,
Portsmouth Road
Bursledon, Southampton,
Hants SO3 8EP
Tel: 0703 404445

Kobashi
50 High St, Ide, Exeter,
Devon EX2 9RW
Tel: 0392 217628

The Sheffield College
428a Ecclesall Road
Sheffield S11 8PX
Tel: 0742 682140

Acu Medic Centre
101-103 Camden High Street,
London NW1 7JN
Tel: 071 388 5783/388 6704
Fax: 071 387 5766
Telex: 269460 ACUMED G

Shirley Price Aromatherapy
College
PO Box 29, Hinckley,
Leicestershire LE10 0FT
Tel: 0455 615466
Fax: 0455 615054

**Springtime Aromatherapy
is pleased to offer ladies
professional advice, aroma-
treatments and Bach flower
remedies in a relaxed
friendly atmosphere
Margaret Maunder ISPA
Tel: Ipswich 612601**

Mrs Margaret Weeds MIFA
MBSR SPA Dip MIPTI ITEC
17 Freckenham Road,
Worlington,
Nr Mildenhall, Suffolk
P28 8SQ
Tel: 0638 716759

Celestial Designs
Aromatherapy
Tan-y-Gyrt Hall
Nantglyn, Nr Denbigh
Clwyd LL16 5DP
Tel: 0745 70411/70308

Alison Mold B Ed (Hons) Dip
BWY (Cert in Remedial Yoga)
Dip SPA ISPA
Natural Choice Therapy
Centre
24 St John Street
Ashbourne, Derbys DE6 1GH
Tel: 0335 46096

Edwina North SEN DoN LLSA
MIFA (Reg)
Natural Choice Therapy
Centre, 24 St John Street
Ashbourne, Derbys DE6 1GH
Tel: 0335 46096

Tobias School of Art

A four-year course
leading to a
diploma in
Artistic Therapy.
Some 3-week blocks
are available on a part-time basis.
Summer courses in July 1994

**Tobias School of Art,
Coombe Hill Road, East Grinstead,
Sussex RH19 4LZ
Telelphone: (0342) 313655**

BAY HOUSE AROMATICS

**296a Ditchling Road
Brighton BN1 6JG
Tel: 0273 559444**

We supply the full range of oils and
other products for aromatherapy.
Everything you need whether you're a complete
beginner or a professional practitioner.
Call in at our friendly aromatic shop in Brighton
or send for our mail order price list and free
introduction to aromatherapy.

Perfection
★ HEALTH & BEAUTY ★
★ Aromatherapy ★ Homoeopathy
★ Magnetic Therapy
★ Beauty Therapy ★ Non Surgical face lift
(by Matis of Paris) ★ Lymphatic drainage
121 Byron Way, Northolt,
Middlesex UB5 6BA
Tel/fax: 081 845 8582

**Manchester School
of Massage**

✣ **INTRODUCTORY & DIPLOMA COURSES** ✣
MASSAGE AROMATHERAPY REFLEXOLOGY SPORTS THERAPY ON SITE MASSAGE SHIATSU

77 RUSSELL ROAD MANCHESTER M16 8AR

TEL: 061 862 9752

Mrs Joyce Frearson SP Dip
AMISPA
Aromatherapy massage.
Cleckheaton, West Yorkshire
Tel: 0274 876621

Mrs Jones
23 Mellor Road,
Cheadlehume, Stockport
Cheshire
Tel: 061 485 4009

Manchester School of
Massage
77 Russell Road,
Manchester M16 8AR
Tel 061 862 9752

Natural Healing Centre
72 Pasture Road, Goole,
North Humberside DN14 6HE
Tel: 0405 769119

The Aroma Therapy Shop
Flat Lane, Kelsall, Cheshire
Telephone: 0829 751810

FREE AROMATHERAPY MAIL ORDER CATALOGUE

Top quality pure essential oils, carrier oils, body massage and bath oils etc. Extensive range of aromatherapy cruelty-free products

Exclusive special offer aromatherapy starter kits
TRADE WELCOME
For details ring now
091 233 1199
or write to
Nature and Body Care
PO Box 1NJ, Newcastle-upon-Tyne NE99 1NJ

ART THERAPY

Art Therapy is practised in many parts of the world, where it has emerged as a special field of therapy which helps people to express themselves and overcome their problems by working with colours as in painting, line as in drawing and form as in modelling.

The artistic process helps them to understand and atune the imbalances and inter-relationships within their own lives. Anyone with severe emotional or psychological problems may benefit. The art work itself has the possibility even unconsciously to heal, just as in all ages true works of art have had a healing capacity.

For further help contact:

Tobias School of Art,
Coombe Hill Road,
East Grinstead,
Sussex RH19 4LZ
Tel: (0342) 313655

ASTON PATTERNING

Aston Patterning was developed by Judith Aston as an integrated system of movement education, bodywork, environmental evaluation and fitness training designed to teach us how we can recover our body's natural unstressed fluidity and grace.

It recognises each person's unique body shape, asymmetries and limitations in a fluid understanding of the body's balance and sees all movement in terms of three dimensional spirals. The importance of our environment and good design or modification of chairs, shoes, beds, etc. is also taught.

Jean Aston has designed a three-piece wedge seat made of covered foam to modify any uncomfortable seating and bring it into line with the more conscious body.

For further help contact:

Ingrid St Clare
Accredited Aston-Patterner
Seminar and sessions
Tel: 0536 725292

ASTROLOGICAL COUNSELLING

The ancient art and science of astrology has long been associated wiht health and holistic being. Many civilisations across the world use astrological information for assessing the causes of disease and to pinpoint methods of healing appropriate to each patient.

Many of the complementary therapies have strong correspondencies with astrology. It has been linked with herbs since Culpepper in 1655 and with Ayurveda for hundreds of years before that.

A natal chart gives an opportunity to study an overview of the whole person, and can stand on its own or be used as an adjunct to other systems of healing.

For further help contact:

British Astrological and
Psychic Society
124 Trefoil Crescent,
Broadfield, Crawley,
W. Sussex RH11 9EZ
Tel: 0293 542326

AUTOGENIC TRAINING

Autogenic Training is a system of easy mental exercises which brings about profound relaxation and relief from the negative effects of stress. The mind is allowed to calm itself by switching off the body's stress response.

Following an individual assessment, the training is taught to small groups of individuals, over eight to ten weeks, with daily practice at home. The exercises involve taking the focus inward and using mental repetition of a sequence of phrases relating to the body in its relaxed state, while remaining the passive observer of the process.

The technique allows the brain's self-righting processes to work without interference, balancing right and left brain activities. This boosts the immune system, bringing about greater emotional balance and creativity.

Developed in Germany over 60 years ago, and thoroughly researched in several countries, Autogenic Training is used by artists, writers, musicians, athletes, doctors, those in business and in the home, pilots and many others. It is used to support and enhance progress in other therapies. It has been clinically applied with good results over a wide range of disorders, including high blood pressure, asthma, muscular pain and tension, heachaches and irritable bowel syndrome. Many people report improvement in sleep disorders anxiety and self confidence.

Once learned, autogenic training is a permanent life skill, an effective preventative method, versatile and adaptable to any lifestyle.

The British Association for Autogenic Training and Therapy, a registered charity, is the registration and supervisory organisation in the UK for maintaining professional standards in the teaching of autogenic training.

For further help contact:

British Association for
Autogenic Training & Therapy
18 Holtsmere Close,
Watford,
Herts WD2 6NG

**Tamara Burnet-Smith
Autogenic Training
Profound Relaxation and
Stress Management taught
in groups and/or indivldually
Non-drug approach to a
wide range of disorders.
Minimal therapist-
dependency promotes
healing
71 Westfield Road,
Caversham,
Reading RG4 8HL
Tel: 0734 479 957**

Dr Alice Greene
MRCGP MF Hom.
Teaches group and individual at 86 Harley Street W1N 1AE Tel: 071 580 4188

Judith Stafford,
The Alternative Therapy Centre, Tamworth, Staffs
Tel: 0827 69374

Elizabeth Lewin,
Autogenic Training and Counselling
31 Wesley Road, Kingsworthy, Winchester
Tel: 0962 880069

Jane Bird RGN
MemLectBAFATT
Watford, Herts
Tel: 0823 675501

Rita Benor
Autogenic Training
Psychotherapy,
Hypnotherapy
Therapeutic Touch
Individuals, couples, families
Stress management workshops
Bishopsteignton, South Devon
Te/fax: 0626 779218

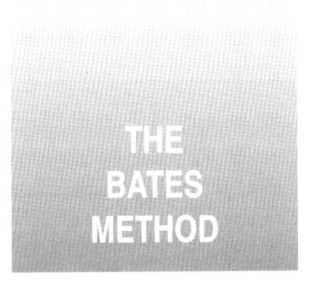

THE BATES METHOD

Poor sight often reflects disturbance of mental, emotional or physical health, or habits of strain which upset the normal co-ordination of mind and body. Teachers of the Bates Method use a broadly holistic approach which seeks to identify the causes of poor vision in the individual case and the most appropriate form of treatment, together with exercises in relaxation, memory, imagination and perception, which are used to improve the feedback between eyes and brain, allowing the eyes to function more normally.

The method has been found helpful in all the conditions for which glasses are normally prescribed and has a long history of success with 'difficult' conditions such as squints and 'lazy eyes'. In combination with suitable therapies, it can also play a valuable supporting role in the healing of eye disease. It is especially valuable as a preventative.

For further help contact:
The Bates Association of Great Britain, Friars Crt, 11 Tarmount Lane,
Shoreham by Sea,
West Sussex BN43 6RQ

Janet Cann. Bates teacher (Member of the Bates Association of Great Britain) sae to: Bath Natural Health Clinic, James Street West, Bath BA1 2BP. Tel: Clinic 0225 313153 (for appointment) Home: 0272 863187

Sheila Parry MSTAT GBC teaches at the Quay Arts Centre, Newport, Isle of Wight and LittleWhitehouse, Whitehouse Cross, Porchfield. For all appointments and information tel: 0983 520211

Anthony Attenborough
128 Merton Road, London SW18 5SP Tel: 081 874 7337

Margaret E Montgomery
Hertfordshire & London W1
For all appointments
tel: 0442 862228

Steven Cooper
10 York Rd, Headington
Oxford OX3 8NW
Tel: 0865 65511 and Bristol House, 80a Southampton Row London WC1B 4BA Tel: 071 404 5348

Chandra Vashisht
49 Old Church Lane,
Stanmore, Middx HA7 2RG
Tel: 081 954 1131

T H Jivraj BSc DHom (Med)
Natural Health Clinic, 286 Preston Rd, Harrow HA3 0QA
Tel: 081-908 4272

David Glassman MSTAT
26 Cleveland Gardens
London NW2 1DY
Tel: 081 455 1317
(also City practice)

BIO FEEDBACK

The body has a problem when it comes to our awareness of our state of health. Generally we are not conscious of most internal processes in our body unless something is wrong. A healthy body gives little feedback whereas a sick body gives feedback of symptoms. Between nothing and symptoms the body provides little information.

Biofeedback removes body blindfolds and brings into consciousness an awareness of how mental and physiological processes interact and how they can be controlled.

Heart rate and blood pressure are monitored routinely by doctors but other parameters such as muscle tension, peripheral skin temperature and skin conductance can be monitored.

Each has its applications in health and in promoting health in ill people.

When you use feedback of biological information to change a bodily function - for instance, muscle tension - you are involved in biofeedback training.

The training implies you learn new skills and change the parameter over time, with practice, using the biofeedback as a guide. As you become more conscious of what you are doing, of what to do and how to do it, your skills improve.

In this way you can control raised blood pressure, headaches, irritable bowel syndrome, neck and back pain plus rehabilitate weak, damaged or chronically tense muscles.

These are just some of the applications of biofeedback (self regulation) training.

For further help contact:

Dr Paul Scarrow
B Med Sci BM BS
Medi-Scene Health Care
Lorelei House,
Old Blyth Road,
Ranby, Retford,
Notts DN22 8HZ
Biofeedback and Muscle Learning Therapy.
See ad under Healthy Living & Well Being
Tel/Fax: 0777 708060

The Awakened Mind Limited
Tel: 081 451 0083

Liongate Clinic

8 Chilston Road, Tunbridge Wells, Kent TN4 9LT
Telephone: 0892 543535

A holistic private medical clinic offering
CHELATION THERAPY and OZONE THERAPY for HEART DISEASE, ARTERIOSCLEROSIS and related conditions

Also at:
Newport, Shropshire 0952 813219
Eastbourne, East Sussex - 0323 734664

The Awakened Mind Limited

Biofeedback instruments...
for hypnotherapists, stress mangagement and relaxation training...
- Professional quality
- our own *Discovery* range
- the Biomonitors ET meter and **Mind Mirror III**

With over 25 years experience in Biofeedback training...
Call us on 081 451 0083

CHELATION THERAPY

Chelation therapy with EDTA, a synthetic amino acid, is a long established method for treating acute lead and other heavy metal poisoning. Its use has been successfully extended to treat all forms of heart disease, angina, peripheral blood vessel disease and their consequences.

Its role as an important preventive health measure, especially in connection with chronic low-level heavy metal exposure (lead, cadmium, aluminium, mercury), the most prevalent pollution burden, is worthy of consideration.

Several long term studies indicate that it may have an important place in the prevention of cancers. It can safely and usefully be combined with ozone therapy and other nutritional or other orthodox and complementary therapies.

For further help contact:
Liongate Clinic
8 Chilston Road, Tunbridge Wells, Kent TN4 9LT
Tel: 0892 543535
Also at:
Newport, Shropshire
Tel: 0952 813219
Eastbourne, East Sussex
Tel: 0323 734664

Dr Elisabeth Dancey BM, 47 Glenview Road, Hemel Hempstead, Herts HP1 1TD
Tel: 0442 235445
Fax: 0442 217979

CHINESE MEDICINE

Chinese medicine has a history of continuous development over the last 2500 years during which time the principles of diagnosis and treatment have been refined.

Chinese medicine comprises:

Chinese herbal medicine, in which herbs are usually combined in formulae or prescriptions tried and tested over the centuries. Their effects are well documented but the art of Chinese herbal medicine is being able to vary the formulae to suit each patient. Herbal medicine is particularly useful in the treatment of chronic conditions which may require treatment over several months and to combat acute infections by eliminating harmful pathogens.

Clinical massage therapy, incorporates a wide variety of techniques, both strong and mild, static and dynamic, including touch, pressure, stretching, manipulation and

Acu Medic CENTRE
101-103 CAMDEN HIGH STREET, LONDON NW1 7JN
TEL: 071 388 5783/388 6704 FAX: 071 387 5766
TELEX: 269460 ACUMED G

assisted exercise.

Acupuncture – see separate section.

Chi-kung, or qi gong is based on the principle that to be truly healthy you must have a healthy physical body and a calm and healthy mind. Many illnesses are caused by imbalances in the mind, for example worry and nerves cause upset stomachs. The gentle but powerful exercise of chi-kung allow the individual to find balance in body and mind.

All these therapies work on very different principles from Western medicine which may seem strange when viewed through mechanistic Western eyes. Yet Chinese medicine is the world's largest medical system serving 1.5 billion people worldwide. It is fully integrated as a medicine in its own right into the public health systems of present-day China and Japan and is recognised by the World Health Organisation.

For further help contact:

Fook Sang Acupuncture and Chinese Herbal Practitioners Training College
1037B Finchley Road,
Golders Green
London NW11 7ES
Tel: 081 455 5508

Acu Medic Centre
101-103 Camden High Street,
London NW1 7JN
Tel: 071 388 5783/388 6704
Fax: 071 387 5766
Telex: 269460 ACUMED G

The Nutri Centre
7 Park Crescent
London W1N 3HE
Tel: 071 436 5122
Fax: 071 436 5171

CHIROPRACTIC

Chiropractic is a gentle way of relieving pain by skilfully manipulating disorders of the joints, muscles and spine.

The consequences of such disorders can include, lumbago, slipped discs, sciatica, and sometimes asthma, arthritis, migraine, period problems and even stress. In many ways, chiropractic is similar to osteopathy as neither therapy uses drugs or surgery, although chiropractors make far greater use of X-rays and conventional diagnostic methods than osteopaths.

Chiropractic can especially help people with whiplash injuries. Many sportsmen suffer from a wide range of injuries that frequently require treatment from chi-

---

FOOK SANG ACUPUNTURE AND CHINESE HERBAL PRACTITIONERS TRAINING COLLEGE

A unique opportunity to acquire correct training in the traditional methods of both Chinese Acupuncture and Chinese Herbal Medicine, enabling future practice with full confidence. Membership for graduates. Courses: Weekends by Chinese Practitioners. Close links with China. Write to:
The Registrar
1037B Finchley Road, Golders Green
London NW11 7ES Tel: 081 455 5508

THE NUTRI CENTRE

SPECIALISTS IN VITAMIN & NUTRITIONAL SUPPLEMENTS

✻ COMPLETE RANGE OF PRACTITIONER PRODUCTS
incl Lamberts, Biocare, Nutriwest, Cytoplan, G & G, Natural Flow, Bio-science, Standard Process, Health Plus, Quest, Solgar, Nutriscene, SHS, Enzyme Process, Cantassium, Nature's Own, NF Products (USA), Thorne and NATREN Probiotics, Blackmores, Healthlink, Advanced Nutrition, Oligoplex, Heel, Dr Reckeweg, Dr Donsbach, Nelson, Ainsworth, Weleda, Pascoe
✻ STOCKISTS OF STANDARD VITAMIN AND NUTRITIONAL SUPPLEMENTS, HOMOEOPATHIC AND BIOCHEMIC REMEDIES, HERBAL AND AYURVEDIC PRODUCTS AND SPECIAL DIETS
✻ EXTENSIVE RANGE OF BOOKS ON HEALTH & COMPLEMENTARY MEDICINE
✻ **MAIL ORDER HOTLINE** 071-426 5122   VAT exemption for Export Sales
All major credit cards accepted   Professional discounts for
orders placed by noon despatched same day   practitioners

ropractors, including strained muscles, sprained joints, damaged ligaments, injured tendons, wrenched knees and tennis elbow.

A first consultation with a chiropractor will result in an examination and X-rays being taken to determine the condition of the spine, which may also reveal signs of arthritis, bone disease or fractures. The chiropractor will then decide whether treatment will help, or if you should rely on a doctor.

For further help contact:

British Chiropractic Association
Premier House, 10 Greycoat Place, London SW1P 1SB
Tel: 0800 212 618

British Association of Applied Chiropractic
PO Box 69, Witney
Oxford OX8 5YD

Complementary Medicine Centre, 9 Corporation Street, Taunton, Somerset TA1 4AJ
Tel: 0823 325022

Philip Greenfield CP AIPc
McTimoney Chiropractor
Natural Choice Therapy Centre, 24 St John Street, Ashbourne, Derbys DE6 1GH
Tel: 0335 346096

Jill Baldwin MA DC (WSC)
Oxfordshire Tel: 0608 810429

Kay McCarroll DHP MC MIPC
McTimoney Chiropractor
Sports Muscle Therapist
The Hendon Practice
12 Golders Rise,
London NW4
Tel: 081 202 9747

COLONIC HYDRO-THERAPY

Colonic hydrotherapy is a safe, effective method of cleansing the colon by gently flushing it with purified water. Most colonic therapists have other complementary medicine training and often will use a range of mutually supporting therapies. Colonic therapy, accompanied by nutritional advice, can help clients affected by constipation, diarrhoea, mucus colitis, colitis, spastic colon, diverticulitis, liver sluggishness, halitosis, headaches and a wide range of common disorders. Chrohn's disease, ME, candida, anorexia and bulimia nervosa can be helped. Side benefits can include an alleviation of PMT.

For further help contact:
Colonic International Assoc
50a Morrish Road,
London SW2 4EG
Tel: 081 671 7136

Susan Fairley MIACT
171 Sandown Road,
Deal, Kent Tel: (0304) 364879

Wholeness
26 Mulberry Way
S Woodford, London
E18 1ED Tel: 081 530 8804
or 071 224 2726

COLOUR THERAPY

Colour therapy, although used by the ancient Egyptians, is still relatively new in Britain. The use of powers of colour can change blood pressure, help respiratory problems, migraine, stress and digestive orders. Consultations are no less than one hour.

Colour therapists will treat any disorder be it mental, emotional, metabolic or physical, but they emphasise that the therapy is complementary to qualified medical treatment, not an alternative.

For further help contact:
Ann Elise Lloyd
Violet Hill Studios,
Centre for Creative Healing,
6 Violet Hill, St John's Wood,
London NW8 9EB
Tel: 071 794 7064
Violet Hill Studios
tel: 071 624 6101

Pauline Wills MIACT HDCTh
MBRA   Tel: 081 204 7672

Susan Fairley MIACT
AURA-SOMA Colour
Therapist. Full programme
of six day Diploma courses
and one day workshops.
171 Sandown Road,
Deal, Kent
Tel: (0304) 364879

COUNSELLING

Counselling is a form of treatment that plays an important role in helping an individual who may be perfectly healthy to deal with a crisis in their lives, such as the death of a close relative or colleague or to improve their lives and relationships.

Counselling can include work with other individuals, pairs or groups of people, where the objectives of particular counselling relationships will vary according to each client's needs.

The counsellor's role is to facilitate the client's work in ways which respect the client's values, personal resources an capacity for self-determination.

The counselling relationship must be entered into voluntarily.

For further help contact:
National Association of Counsellors, Hypnotherapists and Psychotherapists
145 Coleridge Road
Cambridge CB1 3PN

Athena Counselling Services,
Freepost (BR614),
Brighton BN2 2ZZ
Tel: 0273 697376
Fax: 0273 670181

Jean Taylor PhD (MA) BAC
Secure and pleasant environment to explore personal issues.
Relationship, Crisis Counselling, Stress Management.
93 Northcourt Avenue,
Reading RG2 7HG
Tel: 0734 863399

Re-Vision: Centre for Integrative Psycosynthesis.
Professional training and short courses.
Tel: 081 451 2165

T H Jivraj BSc DHom (Med)
Cert in Counselling,
Natural Health Clinic,
286 Preston Road, Harrow,
Middx HA3 0QA
Tel O81-908 4272

Sheila Dainow DCS DTM MSHP
Therapeutic massage practitioner in North London
For details/appointments
081 368 3605
Holistic Treatment for Stress Symptoms and Chronic Tension

Pauline Wills MIACT HDCTh MBRA
Courses on Colour Therapy
and on The Use of Colour with Reflexology
Treatment by appointment
Details: 081 204 7672

CRANIO SACRAL THERAPY
with Thomas Atlee DO MRO MIRCST
Complete courses in exceptionally gentle yet extremely powerful therapy in London and Abroad.
1 year course, 2 year course, Introductory courses in London, Dublin, Belgium, Italy, Canary Islands.
For further information contact: College of Cranio-Sacral Therapy (CCST),
160 Upper Fant Road, Maidstone, Kent ME16 8DJ
Tel: 0622 729311

Bigger & Better *The Dug Out*

probably the most unusual shop in the country. Regular stocks of healing crystals (natural or polished), spheres, eggs, wands, boji stones, tektites, meteorites, moldavite, crystal jewellery. Also wide selection of minurals and fosuals as well as natural stone giftware.
Send for free mail order list enclosing a 24p stamp to:
Merchants Quay
Gloucester Docks GL1 2ER
Telephone: 0452 304142
Open 10-5.30 daily and 11-5 Sunday

CRANIO SACRAL THERAPY

Craniosacral therapy is a subtle and profound healing form. It is a deeply relaxing therapy which assists the body's natural healing processes and helps increase physical vitality and well-being. It is effective in achieving structural change, yet has much wider applications. It works with many levels of disease and pain. Through working in this way, the musculoskeletal system can be encouraged to balance and heal. The nervous system and its control mechanisms can be assisted to a higher level of functioning and organ systems can be helped towards more balanced functioning and healing.

Extremely subtle qualities of touch are used to assist the body in its healing processes in craniosacral therapy. Patterns of tension, strain and physical resistance are encouraged to release and heal, and profound levels of relaxation can be experienced. Congestion and tension in the cranium, nervous system and spine can be encouraged towards greater ease with these very gentle procedures of touch. Nervous system disorders, migraine, respiratory, digestive and elminative problems can all be assisted in their healing processes. It is an extremely effective therapy form which is used to treat the whole body.

For further help contact:
Craniosacral Therapy Association
3 Sandgrove Cottages,
Horsley, Nailsworth,
Gloucestershire GL6 0PS
Tel: 0453 833708

Chando Steiner MA (Cantab)
Violet Hill Studios,
Centre for Creative Healing,
6 Violet Hill, St John's Wood,
London NW8 9EB
Tel: 071 272 4516
Violet Hill Studios
Tel: 071 624 6101

Monica Anthony
LRAM BRCP
Practitioner in Colour Healing,
Hypnotherapy,
Cranio-Sacral Therapy,
Holistic Foot Massage
(Courses also available)
Tel: 071 232 2562

Thomas Atlee DO MRO MIRCST
Primrose Healing Centre,
9 St George's Mews,
London NW1 8XE
Tel: 071 5r86 0148

CRYSTAL HEALING GEM THERAPY

Both emotional health and spiritual well-being are said to be helped by this therapy. Crystals of precious and semi precious stones are believed to contain positive energy or natural resonance which can be channelled through the healer to the sufferer. They act like tuning forks to remind us of our potential for balance and health.

Careful placement of stones for a few minutes on and around the body, holding or meditating with crystals, gently moving gemstones through the aura and subtle bodies, all help to remove stress and improve the quality of life on physical, emotional, mental and spiritual levels.

For further help contact:
The Institute of Crystal and Gem Therapists
2 Kerswell Cottages
Exminster, Exeter, Devon
EX6 8AY

The Dug Out
Merchants Quay
Gloucester Docks GL1 2ER
Telephone: 0452 304182

DANCE MOVEMENT THERAPY

Healing dance is designed to wake the body's own power of healing through connecting to the energy of self, using breathing, movement, meditation, visualisation, rhythm and voice. Movement rituals allows the dancer to become more in touch with the depth of his or her feelings and sensations. New patterns of movement are discovered channelling appropriate images of strength, vitality, joy, balance and release.

Through the power of music, voice and drumming, old, negative patterns can also be let go so that the healing dance can begin with oneself and interaction through contact with others.

For further help contact:
Magda Williams, Kent
Tel:0732 454627

DIETARY THERAPEUTICS

Diet is considered by many alternative practitioners to be one of the most important factors in the prevention of health and disease. A healthy wholefood diet usually consists of fresh fruit and vegetables, beans and peas, small quantities of dairy products, fish, lean meat and poultry, but there are also more specialised diets to effectively treat particular problems.

Low-fat diets are often recommended for patients with angina (hardening of the arteries) or heart disorders, salt-free diets can benefit people with high blood pressure, and for those with bowel disorders a rich fibre diet is important.

For further help contact:

Dr Bob Lawrence,
Dietary Research Limited,
University Innovation Centre,
Singleton Park, Swansea,
West Glam SA2 8PP
Tel: 0792 295562
Fax: 0792 295613

General Designs Ltd
(Pastarisa/Ener-G Foods Distributor)
PO Box 38, Kingston, Surrey
KT2 7YP
Tel: 081 336 2323
See advertisement under the Allergy Therapy section.

Dance-Movement-Therapy

Use your creativity to mobilise your physical, mental and emotional resources. Move towards change.

Magda Williams 0732 454627

THE FELDENKRAIS METHOD

Mark Pfeffer Ph D
291 Cricklewood Lane
London NW2 2JZ
Individual sessions and classes "Discovering and maximising your inherent potential"
Tel: 081 346 0258

FLOATATION THERAPY

The Feldenkrais Method, based on the work of Moshe Feldenkrais (1904-1984), is influenced by Feldenkrais' expertise in physics, engineering and judo. The method uses movement to bring about improved functioning, through 'Awareness Through Movement' group classes and individual 'Functional Integration' lessons. Both types of lessons are appropriate for a wide range of people of all ages and abilities
For further help contact:
The Feldenkrais Guild UK
PO Box 370
London N10 3XA
Tel: 0273 327406

Floatation therapy, or Restricted Environmental Stimulus therapy, is a technique that harmonises the mind, body and spirit by releasing the body from environmental stress and stimulus.

It works be temporarily releasing the body from environmnetal stress and stimulus which triggers the body's natural relaxation responses. The float tank contains a shallow pool of warm water saturated with Epsom salts where the client floats in an atmosphere of complete darkness and tranquility for about an hour.

Users report feelings of

Dietary Research Limited

Leaders in the field of Dietary Therapeutics
- offers an effective dietary treatment for -
arthritis, skin complaints, mutiple sclerosis, myalgic encephalomyelitis, colitis, pre-menstrual syndrome, post-natal depression, hayfever and other allergies, migraine, asthma and eczema.
for FREE information write or telephone:

Dr Bob Lawrence, Dietary Research Limited,
University Innovation Centre, Singleton Park,
Swansea, West Glam SA2 8PP
Tel: 0792 295562 Fax: 0792 295613

FLOATATION
THE SPA TREATMENT OF THE 1990s
Now available at Complementary Medicine Clinic
65 GROSVENOR ROAD, TUNBRIDGE WELLS, KENT
Complementary/Holistic Medicine Practitioners work within the centre offering other alternative therapies. STRESSED, DEPRESSED, ANXIOUS OR FATIGUED? THEN TRY FLOATING FOR TOTAL RELAXATION
(1 hour float is equivalent to 6-8 hours sleep)
Complementary Medicine Clinic has been established to promote natural health and stress management and to bring total relaxation to all who use the many therapies available and who shop within the centre
TEL 0892 518999 FAX 0892 540834
For appointment
Member of The Floatation Tank Association (UK)

increased creativity, and a decrease of stress related symptoms.
For further help contact:
Floatation Tank Assoc (UK)
3a Elms Crescent,
London SW4 8QE

Complementary Health Clinic
65 Grosvenor Road,
Tunbridge Wells, Kent
Tel: 0892 518999
Fax: 0892 540834

Super Lighthouse, Gwent
Real Lighthouse on crossing leylines
Built 1821, Grade II listed.
Superb B&B accommodation, floatation tank & W Reich's orgone accummulator.
Other therapies available.
Peaceful, off the beaten track and different
Tel: 0633 810126/815860

HEALING

Healing by touch is a remarkable yet simple therapy where a gifted individual summons inner powers to fight illness and disease or alleviate pain in a patient.

Some healers believe that their power of healing are channelled through an outside spiritual source that develops in the patient being treated. This is said to restore the patient's balance of energies by bringing about a wonderful sense of well being by promoting relaxation, a quiet confidence in their ability to think well and get well.

Although some medical experts dismiss the work of healers, there are more than 20,000 healers practising in Great Britain today.

For further help contact:

Caroline Palmer
Violet Hill Studio, Centre for Creative Healing,
6 Violet Hill, St John's Wood,
London NW8 9EB
Tel: 081 749 2430
Violet Hill Studios
tel: 071 624 6101

The Springfield Clinic of Natural Healing
Springfield House, Newgate, Wilmslow,
Cheshire SK9 5LL. Healing with a difference.
Tel: 0625 523155.

Natural Healing Centre
72 Pasture Road, Goole,
North Humberside DN14 6HE
Acupuncture . Bach flowers .
Crystal Healing .
Aromatherapy . Chiropody .
Homoeopathy .
Hypnotherapy . Iridology .
Remedial Massage . Eleven years of Natural therapies in Humberside.
We have time to listen
Tel: 0405 769119.

Monica Anthony
LRAM BRCP
Practitioner in Colour Healing, Hypnotherapy, Cranio-Sacral Therapy, Holistic Foot Massage
(Courses also available)
Tel: 071 232 2562

Janet Love NFSH
Healer - Medium - Herbalist.
Stevenage, Herts.
Tel: 0438 369261

Alice Friend
Dove Cottage,
40 Summer Street, Stroud,
Glos GL5 1NT
Tel: 0453 750919

Barbara Lewis
Distance or Contact Healing
28 Erwgoch, Waun Fawr
Aberystwyth, Dyfed
SY23 3AZ
Tel: 0970 623040

HELLERWORK

Hellerwork is an integrating process combining structural bodywork, movement education and dialogue, exploring how your body reflects your mind.

The aim is to become free of set patterns – mental and physical – to enhance your ability to adapt more easily to life's changes, and to allow you to use your body in the best possible manner.

Hellerwork is a 'hands-on' treatment releasing chronic tension and rigidity in your body and bringing in balance and alignment. It helps you to become body aware and gives you new choices in movement, preventing the return of tension. Hellerwork also allows you to recognise how your attitudes, thoughts, beliefs and emotions affect your body, further assisting you to discover new ways of dealing with the stress of life.

Joseph Heller was an aerospace engineer in Pasadena, California. Later he became the director of Kairos, a Los Angeles centre for human development, and participated in year-long trainings in bioenergetics and gestalt.

He became a Rolfer in 1972 and studied with Ida Rolf until 1978, also learning Patterning from Judith Aston. He became the first president of the Rolf Institute in 1976 and left to found Hellerwork in 1978.

For further help contact:
European Hellerwork Training Foundation
c/o Roger Golten
23 The Grove,
Latimer, Chesham,
Bucks HP5 1UE
Tel: 0494 765481

HELLERWORK

HELLERWORK makes a difference

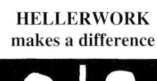

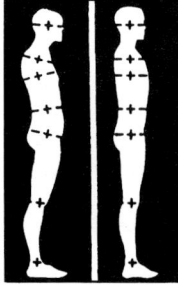

ROSA MARIA AMOROSO
071 247 9982
London EC2
081 539 3923
London E11

KATRIN SIEVERS
010 49 53 71
57675 57433 Fax
Gifhorn Germany

WENDY HELYAR
071 636 5639
London W1
071 402 8613
London W2

DAVID DENE 010
43 53 56 55495
Kitzbuhel, Austria

ROGER GOLTEN
0923 268795
Kings Langley,
Herts
0860 393812
Mobile in London

MS TERRY PETERSON
071 626 3161
London EC2
081 889 1854
London N22

Body stress and tension | Enhanced structural balance

European Professional Training Starts 1994
Contact Practitioners for more information

Alice Friend
(formerly Wilcocks)

Dove Cottage,
40 Summer St,
Stroud,
Glos GL5 1NT

Alice has had experience in medicine wheel work, personal intense therapy, leading workshops, knitting rainbow healing sweaters, writing and bringing up children. She is a trained healer, counsellor and medium. Her work is mainly in mediumship using that as a mirror to reflect answers and unlock the soul's ability to move foward.

Tel: 0453 750919

HERBAL MEDICINE

The medicinal use of herbs can be traced as far back as ancient Egypt, followed by the Greeks and the Roman. Monasteries in mediaeval England each had their own psychic garden where they grew herbs to treat the monks and local people. Primitive rain forest tribes still rely upon their knowledge of the healing properties of plants.

Nicholas Culpeper (1616-54) wrote several books on the subject.

The use of herbal medicine is now widespread and increasing. Patients are treated individually following a physical examination. Herbalist's claim that their medicine can benefit most people suffering from all kinds of illnesses, particularly those with long-standing conditions, such as arthritis and skin disorders.

For further help:

A list of qualified herbalists can be obtained by sending a SAE to The National Institute of Medical Herbalists Ltd., 9 Palace Gate, Exeter, Devon EX1 1JA

Complementary Medicine Centre, 9 Corporation Street, Taunton, Somerset TA1 4AJ
Tel: 0823 325022

Margaret E Pardoe RIr MH SRN SCM registered
Natural Choice Therapy Centre, 24 St John Street, Ashbourne, Derbys DE6 1GH
Tel: 0335 346096

The Springfield Clinic of Natural Healing
Springfield House, Newgate, Wilmslow, Cheshire SK9 5LL.
Healing with a difference.
Tel: 0625 523155.

Mrs N Manston MNIMH
Member of the Register of Osteopaths, 5 Church Street, Beckley, Oxon OX3 9UT
Tel 0865 351784

**The Nutri Centre
7 Park Crescent
London W1N 3HE
Tel: 071 436 5122
Fax: 071 436 5171
Specialists in vitamin and nutritional supplements including practitioners products**

Jacob Briskham BA Hons Member of National Institute of Medical Herbalists CMN-IMH Aylesbury, Bucks Phone for appointment of information at anytime 0296 84394. Including weekends

Ms G Leddy MNIMH
29 Warwick Gardens, Ilford, Essex IG1 4LE
Tel: 081 518 1442

HOMOEOPATHY

More and more doctors and medical students are being attracted to homoeopathy because it enhances the scope and repertoire of their clinical practice. The more obvious advantages are safety, economy and patient satisfaction. Homoeopathic medicines are free from the adverse side effects usually associated with contemporary drugs. They are also very economical.

Homoeopathy is based on the principle that 'like cures like'. Because of its efficacy in the treatment of all kinds of illness, both in the mental and physical spheres by looking for the underlying cause, homoeopathy is a tremendous potential asset in improving the nation's health.

Homoeopathy has been part of the NHS since its inception in 1948 when four hospitals in England and one in Scotland were accorded special status. All currently have very busy out-patient departments. The Bristol Homoeopathic Hospital has to cover demand from Wales which does not have a hospital of its own.

Doctors obtain post graduate training at The Faculty of Homoeopathy which has its seat at the Royal London Homoeopathic Hospital, Great Ormond Street and, in addition, homoeopathic medicine is now being offered at the principal medical school in Glasgow. Veterinary surgeons are also using homoeopathy with great success.

Founded in 1902 by people convinced of the efficacy of homoeopathic medicines, the British Homoeopathic Association is currently presssing for more homoeopathy in the NHS, convinced that this will reduce the incidence of istrogenic disease, reduce costs by cutting short serious illnesses with the absence of serious side and after-effects; convalescence is less prolonged and the results more long lasting. Perhaps the most spectacular result seen from the use of homoeopathy through succeeding generations is the improvement in the all-round health of children.

For further help contact:
British Homoeopathic Association, 27a Devonshire Street, London W1N 1RJ
Tel: 071 935 2163

Kath Chapman
Complex Homoeopathy (Bolton) Ltd, 19 Park St, Bolton BL1 4BD
Tel: 0204 384550

Natural Healing Centre
72 Pasture Road, Goole, North Humberside DN14 6HE
Tel: 0405 769119.

Galen Homoepathics (JA Eiles MPS) Postal Service Available (24 hour Ansaphone Service)
Lewell Mill, West Stafford, Dorchester, Dorset DT2 8AN
Telephone: Dorchester 0305 263996 Fax: 0305 250792

Dr M H Cox MBBS
386 Upper Richmond Rd W, East Sheen, London SW14 7JU Tel: 081 878 3512

Angela Needham MA MCH RSHOM
2 Prospect House, 295 City Road, Sheffield S2 5HH
Tel: 0742 759136

John Coatman MA DSH
Natural Choice Therapy Clinic, 24 St John Street, Ashbourne, Derbyshire DE6 1GH
Tel: 0335 346096

Ainsworths
HOMOEOPATHIC PHARMACY

Remedies by return
24 hour postal service

38 New Cavendish Street, London W1M 7LH
Prescriptions 071 935 5330
Fax: 071 486 4313
Answer phone 071 487 5253

ORDERS ACCOUNTS BOOKS

40-44 High Street, Caterham, Surrey CR3 5UB
Tel: Caterham (0883) 340332
Fax: (0883) 344602

COMPLEX HOMOEOPATHY (BOLTON) LTD

We offer to Professionals the complete range of **Dr Reckeweg's** products.
R1-R95 Complex hand prepared remedies.
CLASSICAL Remedies in various potencies including Tissue Salts and **Biochemic Range**.

We would also like to introduce new additions to Dr Reckeweg's range which are new in stock in England

**REVET - VETERINARY PRODUCTS
EAP - ELECTRICAL ACUPUNCTURE TESTING APPARATUS**
(demonstrations now being given - please telephone for your appointment).

VITAMIN GELEE ROYAL - FOOD SUPPLEMENT
containing pure Royal Jelly with 9 added vitamins

For free information and price list on all our products, please contact:
Kath Chapman, **Complex Homoeopathy (Bolton) Ltd**
19 Park Street, Bolton BL1 4BD
Telephone: 0204 384550 Fax: 0204 384544

Joan Szinay BA LCC HMHMA (UK)
Violet Hill Studios, Centre for Creative Healing,
6 Violet Hill, St John's Wood,
London NW8 9EB
Tel: 081 449 3626
Violet Hill Studios
tel: 071 624 6101

Complementary Medicine Centre 9 Corporation Street,
Taunton, Somerset TA1 4AJ
Tel: 0823 325022

**Mahmood Chaudry
B Pharm (Hons) MR Pharm S D Hon M MRH, Registered Homoeopath. Consultations by appointment only at 46 Greywell Precinct
Leigh Park, Havant
Hants PO9 5AL
Tel: 0705 471781**

Ainsworths Homoeopathic Pharmacy, 38 New Cavendish St, London W1M 7LH
Prescriptions: 071 935 5330
Fax: 071 486 4313
Answer phone: 071 487 5253
and 40-44 High Street,
Caterham, Surrey CR3 5UB
Tel: (0883) 340332
Fax: (0883) 344602

**Dr Alice Greene MB
Bch BAO MRCGP MF Hom. Homoeopathy, counselling, autogenic training.
Fourth Floor Flat, 86 Harley St, London W1N 1AE
Tel: 071 580 4188**

T H Jivraj BSc DHom (Med) Cert in Counselling,
Natural Health Clinic,
286 Preston Road, Harrow,
Middx HA3 0QA
Tel 081-908 4272

HYPNO-THERAPY

Hypnotherapy is the use of hypnosis to attempt alleviation of various symptoms. Its use was frowned upon by the British Medical Association at the turn of the century, but is now recognised as a healing state that allows the mind and body to achieve a calmness in which changes can be made that would otherwise be impossible in a fully conscious state.

Hypnotherapy is not usually offered on the National Health Service because of the timescale incurred by each session, but it is available by private consultation with a psychotherapist.

There are many techniques used by the psychotherapist and of these, hypnosis is the most valuable. Not only does the body relax in the hypnotic state but the barrier that controls the flow of information to and from the unsubconscious mind is also relaxed. The feeling is similar to dozing off to sleep and while in this state a patient can be guided by the psychotherapist to recognise more positive abilities, to view their problems in a better prospective, develop confidence and self-esteem.

Equally, the therapist can give the patient an opportunity to explore traumatic events which may have occurred in the past, allowing them to release the pain and unhappiness associated with it. In doing so it can also permanently release emotional blocks that the patient has found restrictive upon their enjoyment of daily life. It is quite common nowadays for a therapist to teach a patient to undertake self-hypnosis once an illness has been brought under control, particularly asthmatics and insomniacs where frequent help is often required.

**For further help:
British Society of Medical and Dental Hypnosis
The National Office,
17 Keppel View Road,
Kimberworth,
Rotherham, S Yorks
S61 2AR
Enclose an SAE for a list of hypnotherapists in your area**

**British Society of Medical and Dental Hypnosis
Scotland
PO Box 1007,
Glasgow G31 2LE
Tel and fax: 041 556 1606
This society's members are all doctors or dentists who provide treatment throughout Scotland
For information contact above address**

Hypnotherapy Control Board
PO Box 180, Bournemouth BH3 7YR
Tel: 0202 311191 (24 hrs)

Recognised Diploma Course in
ERICKSONIAN HYPNOSIS PSYCHOTHERAPY & NLP
At St Ann's Hospital - London and
Highcroft Hospital - Birmingham
Starting every March and October

British Hypnosis Research is the major training organisation for Ericksonian Hypnosis and NLP for the caring professions and is recognised by Health Authorities and Social Services for funding

* Part Time Weekend Courses
* Practical Skill Based Course
* Supervision with Patients
* Live Demonstrations

British Hypnosis Research, Suite 28,
8 Paston Place, Brighton, BN2 1HA
(0273) 693322

BRITISH SOCIETY OF MEDICAL AND DENTAL HYPNOSIS
For a list of hypnotherapists in your area write to The National Office, 17 Keppel View Road, Kimberworth, Rotherham, S Yorks S61 2AR enclosing a SAE

ANALYTICAL HYPNOTHERAPY
OLIVE BLACKBURN M.I.A.H
Telephone 0202 658578 (24 hrs)
Free introductory consultation and brochure
STOP SMOKING IN ONE SESSION

Angela Needham MA MCH RSHOM Homoeopath.
The safe form of medicine for the future.
2 Prospect House, 295 City Road, Sheffield S2 5HH Clinics on Monday, Tuesday and Thursday. Flexible fees. Enquiries, appointments
Tel: 0742 759136

CENTRE OF INTEGRAL PSYCHOANALYSIS
Health & Personal Growth Psychotherapy
Individual and Group Psychotherapy
How to prevent and deal with emotional and physical diseases with no medicines.

* Free lectures every Monday 7.30pm
* Therapy Workshop every Thursday 7.30pm

6 Colville Road, London W11 2BP
Telephone 071 727 4404 Notting Hill

COMPLEMENTARY MEDICINE SERVICES
(incorporating the Allergy Centre)
9 CORPORATION STREET
TAUNTON, SOMERSET TA1 4AJ
Tel: 0823 325022

Do you need help with recurrent health problems?
For example Candida (thrush), Cystitis, Irritable Bowel, Allergies, Fluid Retention, Hyperactivity (children), Stress, Migraine, Pre-menstrual Syndrome etc.
Come and talk to us we are right next to the library

Our practitioners are fully qualified and they are always happy to spend 10 minutes discussing a particular problem with you prior to making an appointment

● Acupuncture ● Aromatherapy ● Chiropodists
● Allergy therapy ● Food allergy testing ● Herbal medicine ● Holistic massage ● Hypnotherapy ● Homoeopathy
● Iridology ● Osteopathy ● Psychotherapy ● Reflexology
● Shiatsu ● Vitamin & mineral deficiency testing

HYPNOTHERAPY PSYCHOTHERAPY COUNSELLING

Train for the professional qualification or study for interest.

● Accredited by The British Accreditation Council for Independent Further and Higher Education.
● Weekend study courses established in London, Cheshire, Glasgow and elsewhere in the UK
● All courses under the guidance of qualified and established practitioners
● Established for over a decade, the National College is the sole training faculty for the National Register of Hypnotherapists and Psychotherapists, and a recognised training faculty for the British Register of Complemenatry Practitioners (Hypnotherapy), founded at our initiative.
● Both the National College and Register are founder members of the United Kingdom Standing Conference for Psychotherapy
● Supplies external tutors to Royal College of Nursing Institute of Advanced Nursing Education/Royal College of Nursing

For prospectus, send 2x2nd class stamps to:
The National College of Hypnosis and Psychotherapy
12 Cross Street, Nelson, Lancs BB9 7EN
Telephone: (0282) 699378
Fax: (0282) 698633

The National College of
Hypnosis and Psychotherapy
12 Cross Street,
Nelson, Lancs BB9 7EN
Tel: 0282 699378
Fax: 0282 698633

The Complementary Health
Practice
Newcastle-under-Lyme
Tel: 0782 7123127
Harley Street
Tel: 071 636 6540

Olive Blackburn MIAH
Tel: 0202 658578 (24 hrs)
British Hypnosis Research,
Suite 28, 8 Paston Place,
Brighton, BN2 1HA
Tel: 0273 693622

Mrs Jones
23 Mellor Road,
Cheadlehume, Stockport
Cheshire
Tel: 061 485 4009

Dr John M Plowman PhD DHP
(NC) MNRHP
Caerleon Centre of
Hypnotherapy and
Psychotherapy
22 Goldcroft Common,
Caerleon, Gwent NP6 1NG
Tel: 0633 420095

Complementary Medicine
Centre 9, Corporation Street,
Taunton, Somerset TA1 4AJ
Tel: 0823 325022

Natural Healing Centre
72 Pasture Road, Goole,
North Humberside DN14 6HE
Tel: 0405 769119.

**Mrs Dawson
Reflexology, Holistic
Massage and Hypnotherapy**
Loughton, Essex
Tel: 081 508 2553

Stuart Wetherell DHP MAPT
Hypnotherapist &
Counsellor, Essex
Working with people –
to help them. Over 17 years
in helping professions.
Specialising in anxiety
related problems; also habit
reform, relationships,
performance, motivation etc.
Member British Register of
Complementary
Practitioners (Hyp)
Tel: 0245 262975

Monica Anthony LRAM BRCP
Practitioner in Colour Healing,
Hypnotherapy, Cranio-Sacral
Therapy, Holistic Foot
Massage (Courses available)
Tel: 071 232 2562

Under the auspices of the
Association of Qualified
Curative Hypnotherapists.
Practical weekend courses
commence each spring and
autumn for those who
successfully pass the 3
month home-study section.
Full details write or phone
Therapy Training College,
8 & 10 Balaclava Road,
Kings Heath,
Birmingham B14 7SG
Tel: 021 444 5435

Elizabeth J Bowman
British Register of
Complementary
Practitioners (Hypnotherapy)
RMN Dip Thp MSAPP CRAH
N-SHAP UKCC.
Hypnotherapy,
psychotherapy, counselling
for all relationship problems,
emotional difficulties,
smoking, natural weight
loss, eating disorders,
migraine, children/teenagers
behavioural and learning
difficulties, lack of
confidence, exam nerves.
Tel: 0825 732273 (E Sussex)
Qualified Practitioners
Therapeutic Hypnosis

THE COMPLEMENTARY HEALTH PRACTICE

Natural healing in conjunction with complementary and orthodox therapies provides a truly holistic approach to good health.
Treatments include manipulation, acupuncture, massage (remedial and aromotherapy), hypnotherapy, reflexology, allergy testing, homoeopathy, herbalism.

For more details and appointments telephone:
**Newcastle-under-Lyme 0782 712127
Harley Street 071 636 6540**

DR JOHN PLOWMAN

Caerleon Centre of Hypnotherapy & Psychotherapy
Dr John M Plowman, Ph D, DHP (NC) MNRHP
Member of: The National Register of Hypnotherapists & Psychotherapists, The British Psychological Society The National Assoc. of Teachers in Further & Higher Education.

STRESS ● WEIGHT ● SMOKING
PHOBIAS ● SPORTS THERAPY
SELF GROWTH ● EDUCATIONAL COUNSELLING

For Confidential & Qualified Consultations

Tel: Newport (0633) 420095
By appointment only
22 Goldcroft Common
Caerleon, Gwent NP6 1NG

INTEGRAL PSYCHO-ANALYSIS

Integral Psychoanalysis is a short term psychotherapy that deals with the human being as a whole - mind, body and spirit, feeling, thought and action.

Integral psychoanalysis considers pathology as the erroneous and corrupted use of the will, a mechanism of which the individual adopts attitudes of envy and arrogance, as opposed to reality.

Every person - however sick he or she appears - has sanity as a natural basis. He becomes ill in order to refuse the consciousness of what he is. He ends by corrupting, attacking and sabotaging his own life and that of others.

Psychoanalysis aims to help these individuals.

For further help contact:
Centre of Integral Pyschoanalysis
6 Colville Road,
London W11 2BP

Margaret Pardoe RIr MH SRN SCM
Natural Choice Therapy
Centre 24 St John Street,
Ashbourne, Derbyshire
DE6 1GH
Tel: 0335 346096

IRIDOLOGY

Iridology is a form of diagnosis. By analysing inherited markings in the iris of the eye, the iridologist is able to determine genetic strengths and potential weakness of an individual. Most symptoms do not just appear - they are the result of your genetic inheritance and are seen in the iris.

Each person's iris is a unique pattern of colour and structure, like a fingerprint, and is totally unique to each person. Because the iris does not change in structure, it remains a constant source of health information ready to be viewed with magnification and illumination by professional iridologists.

The Society of Iridologists runs a one year professional training course in iridology. Registered iridologists use the initials R Ir after their name. Ensure your practitioner is registered.

For further help contact:
Society of Iridologists
998 Wimbourne Road,
Moordown,
Bournemouth BH9 2DE
Tel: 0202 518078

National Council and Register of Iridologists
80 Portland Road
Bournemouth BH9 1NQ

Complementary Medicine
Centre 9 Corporation Street,
Taunton, Somerset TA1 4AJ
Tel: 0823 325022

Margaret Pardoe RIr MH SRN SCM
Natural Choice Therapy
Centre, 24 St John Street,
Ashbourne, Derbyshire
DE6 1GH
Tel: 0335 346096

Natural Healing Centre
72 Pasture Road, Goole,
North Humberside DN14 6HE
Tel: 0405 769119.

KINESIOLOGY

Kinesiology uses a combination of concepts and techniques drawn from acupuncture, chiropractic, massage, nutrition, osteopathy, shiatsu and others.

Its eclectic approach forms a very useful toolkit for practitioners of all types to use in conjunction with their other skills.

Kinesiology uses simple muscle tests to analyse functional imbalances in the body, and uses touch acupressure, massage and nutritional support to resolve them.

The therapy was created in 1964 by Dr George Goodheart, a chiropractor, who found that by testing muscles and correcting those functioning below par, he could obtain instantaneous improvements.

Research continued and when the meridians of acupuncture were correlated to the muscles, this created a breakthrough which led to a much greater understanding of physiological functions, their electro-magnetic control circuits and bio-computer functions.

For further help contact:

The Academy of Systematic Kinesiology
39 Browns Road,
Surbiton, Surrey KT5 8ST
Tel: 081 399 3215

Jacqueline Beacon Edu K TFH
Violet Hills Studios,
Centre for Creative Healing,
6 Violet Hill, St John's Wood,
London NW8 9EB.
Tel: 081 455 7912
Violet Hill Studios
tel: 071 624 6101

Alison Perrott SP Dip A,
MISPA, MISMA, MASK, MTMI,
The S.E.E.D Institute,
10 Magnolia Way, Fleet,
Hants GU13 9JZ
Tel: 0252 626448
See ad under Courses

KINESIOLOGY
MUSCLE TESTING & ENERGY BALANCING
FOR
BALANCED HEALTH
THE BEST WAY TO LEARN TO USE KINESIOLOGY IS WITH EXPERTS

PRACTITIONERS FIND A.K ANALYSIS QUICK AND EASY TO USE, SIMPLE TO INCORPORATE IN PRACTICE

NON-INTRUSIVE TESTS REVEAL MUSCULO-SKELETAL PROBLEMS
DIETARY DEFICIENCIES

FEARS, PHOBIAS, AND EMOTIONAL AND LEARNING DIFFICULTIES ARE USUALLY QUICKLY RESOLVED

For details of classes and Certified Courses, SAE to:
The Academy of Systematic Kinesiology
39, BROWNS ROAD, SURBITON,
SURREY, KT5 8ST

Manchester School of Massage
✤ INTRODUCTORY & DIPLOMA COURSES ✤
77 RUSSELL ROAD, MANCHESTER M16 8AR
TEL: 061 862 9752

INDIAN HEAD MASSAGE

Head massage has been practised in India for over a thousand years. The technique was originally used by women who believed that massaging their heads with natural oils kept their long hair in healthy and lustrous condition.

Head massage is an excellent treatment also for men. It helps to alleviate stress and tension and for stress linked troubles such as headache, neck ache and eye strain. It soothes, comforts and rebalances energy flow, leaving you with a feeling of peace and well being.

Most important is the impact it has on relationships. As Mr Mehta puts it: "Learning head massage will help your friends ... and those who become your friends. The head and hair are sensitive and touching them is pleasant and soothing. It is one of the ways we know if someone loves and cares for us – that is, by the way they touch our head and hair."

The treatment relieves physical tension and also works on the body's subtle energy to rebalance the whole person.

A weekend course teaches this traditional system. Anyone can learn it, a readily available therapy at your fingertips.
Further information:
Mr Mehta, BA LCSP MCO, DO
Telephone: 071 609 3590/607 3331

Michael Boyce, Kinesiologist
55 Weatherby, Dunstable,
Beds LU6 1TP
Tel: 0582 665348
Kinesiology may help to alleviate allergic, identify nutitional needs, manage stress, ease phobias, addictions, learning difficulties, relieve back/muscle problems, aches & pains, migraine, headaches. etc.

Rosemary Cunningham BA SRN ITEC FSMT, Essex
Tel: 0702 72459

**Rachel Stanford
LCSP (Assoc) IPII
Remedial Massage.
Touch for Health/
Kinesiology. Therapies for all ages
The Guildhall Treatment Room, 55 Church Street, Eye, Suffolk IP23 7BD
Telephone: 0379 870938**

H Simpson, DO NCSO, MGO(Lon), MICAK, MRSH, MHPA, MAA, MCKORE
Merseyside Tel: 0744 883787

**Kay McCarroll DHP MC MIPC
Kinesiology Instructor
Therapist for TFH Dyslexia Sports and Stress Problems
The Hendon Practice
12 Golders Rise
London NW4
Tel: 081 202 9747**

**Mrs Terry Larder (MIIR MAR ASK) Kinesiologist and Reflexologist
Middle England School of Kinesiology,
81 Lancashire St, Melton Rd, Leicester LE4 7AF
Tel: 0533 661962**

MASSAGE

Massage has been practised in various ways in many cultures for thousands of years.

Massage can be a pleasure both to receive and to give.

It can soothe, heal, invigorate and tone. It helps tired muscles to rest and tight, overworked muscles to relax. Massage doesn't only work on the body - having a massage can benefit mind, body and spirit. The touch and movement of the practitioner's hands helps to relax while this same touch and movement induces deeper breathing greater peace. This can lessen the symptoms of stress and promote better functioning of the immune system through the healing quality of positive touch.

For further help contact:
Association of Massage Practitioners
101 Bounds Green Road,
London N22 4DF

Complementary Medicine Centre 9 Corporation, Street, Taunton, Somerset TA1 4AJ
Tel: 0823 325022

The Edinburgh School of Natural Therapy and Massage,
2 London Street. EH3 6NA
Tel: 031 557 3901

Rachel Stanford LCSP (Assoc) IPII, Remedial Massage.
Touch for Health/
Kinesiology. Therapies for all ages. Guildhall Treatment Room, 55 Church Street, Eye, Suffolk IP23 7BD
Tel: 0379 870938

Alison Perrott Sp DipA, MISPA, MISMA, MASK, MTMI,
The S.E.E.D Institute,
10 Magnolia Way, Fleet, Hants GU13 9JZ Tel: 0252 626448
See ad under Courses

**Shelia Dainow
DCS DTM MSHP Therapeutic Massage Practitioner in London N11 1BT.
For details/appointments
tel: 081 368 3605.
Holistic Treatment for Stress Symptoms & Chronic Tension**

The Churchill Centre
22 Montague Street,
London W1H 1TB
Tel: 071 402 9475

Christine Hudson BA ITEC AIPTI
Natural Choice Therapy Centre, 24 St John Street, Ashbourne, Derbys DE6 1GH
Tel: 0335 346096

Derek Pollard PLD ITEC AIPTI
Natural Choice Therapy Centre 24 St John Street, Ashbourne, Derbys DE6 1GH
Tel: 0335 346096

**Rosemary Cunningham
BA SRN ITEC FSMT, Essex
Holistic massage and sports massage Tel: 0702 72459**

Essex School of Massage
Principal: Jacky Barrett.
Intensive course leading to
professional ITEC
qualification. Small classes.
For details
telephone: 0992 892110

The School of Oriental
Massage
8 Paston Place,
Brighton BN2 1HA
Tel: 0273 693622

Marea Young-Taylor
ITEC AIPTI
For relaxing therapeutic
massage by qualified
therapist. Central London
Tel: 071 262 1426

Mrs Margaret Weeds MIFA
MBSR SPA Dip MIPTI ITEC
17 Freckenham Road,
Worlington, Nr Mildenhall,
Suffolk IP28 8SQ
Tel: 0638 716759

Nature Care School of
Massage, Essex
Tel: 0268 565872

Mrs Jones
23 Mellor Road,
Cheadlehume, Stockport
Cheshire
Tel: 061 485 4009

Judith Stafford,
The Alternative Therapy
Centre, Tamworth, Staffs
Tel: 0827 69374

Enrico Dodson, 21 Cowlersley
Lane, Cowlersley,
Huddersfield HP4 5TY
Tel: 0484 641982

T H Jivraj BSc DHom (Med)
D Acupressure, Cert in
Counselling,
Natural Health Clinic,
286 Preston Road, Harrow,
Middx HA3 0QA
Tel O81-908 4272

The Nutri Centre
7 Park Crescent
London W1N 3HE
Tel: 071 436 5122
Fax: 071 436 5171

New Horizon Aromatics
Christopher G Ockendon
MISPA ITEC
Massage, Aromatherapy,
Reflexology, Naturopath
Horizon House,
Portsmouth Road
Bursledon, Southampton,
Hants SO3 8EP
Tel: 0703 399664

Midlands School of Massage
Nottingham
Tel: 0602 472263

Manchester School of
Massage
77 Russell Road,
Manchester M16 8AR
Tel 061 862 9752

Mrs Dawson
Reflexology, Holistic
Massage and Hypnotherapy
Loughton, Essex
Tel: 081 508 2553

Rosemary Cunningham BA SRN ITEC
FSMT Holistic massage
and sports massage
Tel: 0702 72459

Learn to Massage
The gift of helping others to overcome stress can be yours. We offer weekend, day and evening courses in massage technique up to recognised ITEC Qualification
Full details from: The Churchill Centre
22 Montague Street, London W1H 1TB
Telephone: 071 402 9455

LEARN MASSAGE

AROMATHERAPY   SPORTS THERAPY
REFLEXOLOGY   ITEC DIPLOMA
NATURE CARE SCHOOL OF MASSAGE

Tel: 0268 565872
For Prospectus

Diploma in
TRADITIONAL THAI HEALING MASSAGE

in Hospitals around the country
For full detailed brochure contact:

The School of Oriental Massage
8 Paston Place, Brighton BN2 1HA
Tel: 0273 693622

MEDITATION

To benefit fully from meditation, it must be practised wholeheartedly and regularly to bring peace of mind and relaxation. Worries and anxieties decrease and there is a better sense of proportion. Efficiency and confidence increase, relationships are often easier and life seems more purposeful.

Scientific experiments on people meditating have found a general reduction in breathing and heart rate. The basal metabolic rate can decrease by as much as 40 per cent and brain impulses indicate a state of deep rest more profound than sleep or hypnosis – but combined with an inner alertness.

For further help contact:
The School of Meditation
158 Holland Park Avenue,
London W11 4UH
Tel: 071 603 6116

Alison Perrott SP DipA,
MISPA, MISMA, MASK, MTMI,
The SEED Institute,
10 Magnolia Way, Fleet, Hants
GU13 9JZ tel: 0252 626448
See ad under Courses

Jean Taylor PhD (MA) BAC
Groups from beginners onwards. Counselling, Healing, Workshops, Guided Visualisations, Stress Relief.
93 Northcourt Avenue,
Reading RG2 7HG
Tel: 0734 863399

Ingrid St Clare
**Transcendental energy science.
Simple easy method**
Tel: 0536 725292

DIRECTION

Living and travelling in the city every day as most of us do, it's easy to think of places we'd rather be and things we'd rather be doing.

However, there is an inner resource available which provides direction and enables us to come to terms with our surroundings and the people around us, without the desire escape. We feel less frustrated and concerned by events beyond our control. Then, with inner stability and quiet assurance, life becomes happier and more fulfilling.

The simple technique of meditation gives direction to this natural state of being.

If you would like to know more about meditation, the School holds regular introductory meetings on the 1st and 4th Thursday and 3rd Sunday of each month. There are exceptions at Christmas, Easter and during July and August so please telephone to check at these times.

Meetings start at 7.30pm Admission 60p
For private appointments please telephone

The School of Meditation

158 Holland Park Avenue, London W11 4UH
Nearest tube station: Holland Park

Telephone 071 603 6116

MEGAVITAMIN THERAPY

Megavitamin therapy is an extension of corrective diet therapy where individuals are assessed on their personal vitamin and mineral needs. Even with a healthy diet, patients may not receive enough vitamins and minerals because their bodies are unable to absorb them. This particularly applies to cancer sufferers. The situation is rectified by megavitamin therapy which allows much larger amounts of vitamins to be given, well exceeding the normal recommendations.

Megavitamin therapy is most commonly and effectively used with nutrition therapy.

For further help contact:
The Nutri Centre
7 Park Crescent
London W1N 3HE
Tel: 071 436 5122
Fax: 071 436 5171
Specialists in vitamin and nutritional supplements including practitioners products

MESOTHERAPY

Mesotherapy is a medical technique of French origin available only to doctors. It has been practised abroad for over 30 years by GPs and hospital doctors and is considered routine and conventional.

Rather like acupuncture, disease or damage to the body is treated according to a number of points on the skin that refer to the source of the disease or damage. These points can be determined by careful examination of the patient and it is into these points that classical medication, in small doses, is injected.

Very short needles are used to deliver minute doses into the dermis just under the skin.

This area acts as a reservoir and slowly releases the active medication to the target tissue. Vitamins, circulation-improving vasodilators, muscle relaxants, calcitonin (calcium regulating hormone), tissue healers and other medication are used according to the type and stage of the disease. Anti-inflammatory agents are rarely used and steroids never.

Pain relief is obtained by the improvement of the underlying condition and is often remarkable. Blood supply to the diseased tissue, so often impaired, can be improved, thereby allowing optimum tissue nutrition, oxygenation and hence, healing. In most cases three or four weekly treatments is sufficient.

Mesotherapy is used to treat diseases hitherto considered chronic such as arthritis, joint pain, back pain, fluid retention, sports injuries, leg ulcers, poor circulation, cellulite, migraine, leg cramps and other degenerative diseases and cases of poor healing.

For further help contact:

Dr Elisabeth Dancey BM Soton
Diplome Belge de la Sante,
Membre de la Societe Belge de Mesotherapie
47 Glenview Road,
Hemel Hempstead,
Herts. HP1 1TD
Tel: 0442 235445
Fax: 0442 217979
Wimpole Street Medical Centre
55 Wimpole Street, London W1M 7DF
Tel: 071 224 1330

Dr Elisabeth Dancey
BM, Diplome Belge de la Sante. Membre Societe Belge de Mesotherapie
Clinics London and Southampton
0703 332919 Andover 0264 358760,
Christchurch 0202 473210

METAMORPHIC TECHNIQUE

Instead of concentrating on symptoms or difficulties, the Metamorphic Technique practitioner acts as a catalyst – touching the spinal reflex points on the feet, hands and head lightly to provide the client with an inner environment free of direction, interference and preconceived ideas so that their own innate intelligence can move their life energy in the way that is necessary, directing them to what feels right– perhaps a new diet or a change in work environment, physical exercise or the right therapy.

Because of its simplicity and the fact that a session is usually very pleasant and relaxing, many people are happy to use this technique every week as a tool for transformation and realisation of their potential.

For further help contact:
The Metamorphic Association
67 Ritherdon Road,
Tooting, London SW17 8QE
Tel: 081 672 5951

Maureen Muschamp
Natural Choice Therapy
Centre, 24 St John Street,
Ashbourne, Derbyshire
DE6 1GH
Tel: 0335 346096

MUSCLE LEARNING THERAPY

Stress causes muscle tension which can result in headaches, neck and backache, and other muscular pains. If this muscle tension becomes habitual and a learned response, the muscle cannot relax but stays partially contracted. Tense muscles become fatigued, there is poor release of metabolites and inflammation develops. These consequences cause muscular pains and even misalignment of the spine or tilting of the pelvis as the partially contracted muscles constantly pull the body away from is natural posture.

Muscle Learning Therapy is a means of identifying this tension and then learning how to relax the muscle in all situations. By placing sensors over the respective muscle, their electrical activity (EMG) is displayed on a large monitor and the client can see, through biofeedback, the degree of tension. The client is an active participant in the therapy, they are taught how to relax these muscles in static and dynamic situations. The skills they acquire can be used in everyday situations to prevent recurrence of the tension without future use of the feedback equipment, or resorting to drug therapy.

Muscle Learning Therapy can be applied to teaching an awareness of weak muscles and how to develop strength, voluntary control and relaxation of these muscles. A prime example of applying this technique of strengthening weak muscles is for people suffering form incontinence.

For further help contact:

Dr Paul Scarrow
Medi-Scene Health Care
Lorelei House,
Old Blyth Road,
Ranby, Retford,
Notts DN22 8HZ
Tel 0777 708060

Dr Paul Scarrow B Med Sci BM BS
Medi Scene Health Care – In the pursuit of Health and Wellness

Lorelei House, Old Blyth Road, Ranby, Retford, Notts DN22 8HZ
Tel & Fax No 0777 7080600

we offer you a comprehensive health and wellness service which addresses your area of concern helping you achieve an improved quality of life

MUSIC, SOUND AND VOICE THERAPIES

For centuries music has been closely associated with healing by allowing us to express a whole range of different mental and physical emotions that could otherwise cause permanent psychological damage if it were bottled up.

It is these responses and expressions that music therapists – of which there are several hundred operating in Britain today – can observe and work with.

Research has also shown that music therapy is a safe and very effective form of treatment. Sound and voice therapy allows individuals to co-ordinate both speech and movement, particularly the physically handicapped who may need to improve their movement or breath control.

For further help contact:
Association of Professional Music Therapists
The Meadow, 68 Pierce Lane,
Fulbourn, Cambs CB1 5DL

British Society for Music Therapists
69 Avondale Avenue, East Bernet, Herts EN4 8NB

Sound Body Sound Mind Sound Spirit Voice and Movement
Workshops to experience the joy of your true self and restore your inner harmony.
Information: 081 579 9664

Ingrid St Clare
The radiant voice with transcendental techniques
Workshops London and regions
Tel: 0536 725292

NEURO LINGUISTIC PROGRAMMING

Neuro-Linguistic Programming has become widely known as a source of surprisingly effective interpersonal communication skills. It developed originally from the work of John Grinder and Richard Bandler, who worked with three leading psychotherapists.

Modelling out the intuitive skills of these therapists, and making them explicit, has led to the development of a comprehensive range of client-centred skills and techniques for enabling people to make changes more easily, quickly and reliably. For example, the phobia cure process can usually help someone to desensitise a phobia in under 15 minutes.

Although the roots of

John Seymour Associates
Britains longest established NLP Training Company

Britain's best selling NLP book
"Introducing Neuro-Linguistic Programming"

Courses in London and Bristol

To order book and free brochure contact:

John Seymour Associates
(0272) 557827

THE NUTRI CENTRE
SPECIALISTS IN VITAMIN & NUTRITIONAL SUPPLEMENTS

✻ COMPLETE RANGE OF PRACTITIONER PRODUCTS
incl Lamberts, Biocare, Nutriwest, Cytoplan, G & G, Natural Flow, Bio-science, Standard Process, Health Plus, Quest, Solgar, Nutriscene, SHS, Enzyme Process, Cantassium, Nature's Own, NF Products (USA), Thorne and NATREN Probiotics, Blackmores, Healthlink, Advanced Nutrition, Oligoplex, Heel, Dr Reckeweg, Dr Donsbach, Nelson, Ainsworth, Weleda, Pascoe
✻ STOCKISTS OF STANDARD VITAMIN AND NUTRITIONAL SUPPLEMENTS, HOMOEOPATHIC AND BIOCHEMIC REMEDIES, HERBAL AND AYURVEDIC PRODUCTS AND SPECIAL DIETS
✻ EXTENSIVE RANGE OF BOOKS ON HEALTH & COMPLEMENTARY MEDICINE
✻ MAIL ORDER HOTLINE 071-426 5122   VAT exemption for Export Sales
All major credit cards accepted   Professional discounts for
orders placed by noon despatched same day   practitioners

neuro-linguistic programming are profound, the basic idea is simple. Human experience is something that we each construct. Once we know how we make up our experience, it becomes a lot easier to make it up the way we would like it to be. Because NLP skills are effective, the field continues to grow rapidly. Personal development is one of the main areas of application. To find out more about it, read *Introducing Neuro-Linguistic Programming* by Joseph O'Connor and John Seymour.
For further help contact:
Association of Neuro-Linguistic Programming
27 Maury Road,
London N16 7BP
Tel: 0384 443935

John Seymour Associates
17 Boyce Drive
St Werberghs Bristol B52 9XQ
Tel: 0272 557827

NATURAL BEAUTY

A balanced diet, regular exercise, satisfying sleep and good relationships are at the core of looking good. But skin care products made from natural ingredients can add the final glow of health.

As the skin has a fluid structure which is acid, fruit acids combined with other plant substances tend to be the kindest to skin.

As we grow older, skin cell renewal slows down and the build up of dead cells can make the complexion look dull. By stimulating the acid mantle, dead skin cells are gently removed each day to reveal the healthy functioning skin below. Cell renewal is achieved by cleansing and using moisturising and treatment creams to nourish and protect. They should not include any chemical dyes, perfumes or preservatives that can cause allergies.
For further help contact:
The Nutri Centre
7 Park Crescent
London W1N 3HE
Tel: 071 436 5122
Fax: 071 436 5171
Specialists in vitamin and nutritional supplements including practitioners products

NUTRITIONAL THERAPY

Health is not just an absence of disease, it's an abundance of well being that depends on food, environment, fitness and state of mind. Lack of basic nutrients can cause skin problems, loss of energy, frequent colds, aching joints, poor concentration, even depression.

Nutritional therapy assesses indiviual needs and provides a personal dietary and nutritional supplement programme.
For further help contact:
Institute for Optimum Nutrition
5 Jerdan Place,
Fulham, London SW6 1BE
Tel: 071 385 7984

The Nutri Centre
7 Park Cres,London W1N 3HE
Tel: 071 436 5122
Fax: 071 436 5171
Specialists in vitamin and
 nutritional supplements

T H Jivraj BSc DHom (Med)
Natural Health Clinic,
286 Preston Road, Harrow,
Middx HA3 0QA
Tel 081-908 4272

H Simpson, DO NCSO,
MGO(Lon), MICAK, MRSH,
MHPA, MAA, MCKORE
Merseyside Tel: 0744 883737

THE NUTRI CENTRE HALE CLINIC 7 PARK CRESENT LONDON W1N 3HE Tel: 071-436 5122 / 071-631 0156

The Nutri Centre is located on the lower ground floor of the Hale Clinic in 7 Park Cresent, London W1N 3HE. The Prestigious (Nash Terrace) cresent is only a few minutes away from underground stations at Great Portland Street, Regents Park and Baker Street.

Clients are often faced with a dilemma when they have been prescribed or recommended a course of nutritional regime by their practitioner or Nutritionist. One often doesn't even know where to begin to find a company which provides all the products he or she needs. It may mean placing orders with a number of different manufacturers whose despatch times vary. Consequently the institution of the regime is delayed or becomes staggered. Since delay can cause upset to someone already in distress and staggering can mean that it takes longer for the full benefit of the treatment to be effected and felt (nutrients interact with each other and the regime will have been designed with this in mind) the client may lose heart and motivation. In an effort to circumvent some of these problems some practitioners have arrangements with certain manufacturer's or else stock the remedies themselves. But time spent in administering the purchase and sale of remedies simply increases the stress load on practitioners and their practices.

For those who do not wish to see a practitioner for any specific illness, there is a problem of trying to obtain professional advice on the use of vitamins and nutritional products to supplement their diet.

The aim of the recently opened NUTRI CENTRE at the Hale Clinic, London, is to lift all these burdens from practitioners and clients. Essentially it stocks or has access to the largest stock of nutritional supplements – from those you would find in a health food shop, to practitioner products, to exclusive lines, even to the occasional batch made up for specific requirements.

Now clients can visit or contact the Nutri Centre knowing that it can almost certainly provide all the products that have been recommended. And if, with this relative ease of availability a client begins to feel better sooner, the incentive to keep going with the regime becomes stronger and healing is achieved at a much faster rate.

Suitably qualified staff are also available to give professional advice on improving compliance of the regime to maximise its therapeutic benefits.

The Nutri Centre operates a prompt and reliable mail order service for those not fortunate to live or work within striking distance, and next day delivery is guaranteed. This service can also be extended to ordering "repeats" enabling them to maintain continuity of the Dietary Supplementation Therapy. The intention, therefore, is that clients from anywhere in the country should be able to order their supplies from just one phone call to the centre.

"The Nutrition Centre's influence on the industry as a whole will be considerable, and indeed, it's already leading the way in a number of areas..."
Jande Vries (June 1991).

COMPLETE RANGE OF PRACTIONER PRODUCTS

Exclusive distributors of Scientific Consulting Services Products (USA), N.F Products (USA), Thorne Research Products (USA) and NATREN Probiotics (USA).

Lamberts	Blackmores	Health Plus	Oligoplex
Nutri-West	Healthlink	Quest	Agnolyt
Biocare	Natures Own	Solgar	Heel
G&C	Cantassium	Lewis	Dr.Reckeweg
Natural Flow	Nature's Plus	Bio-Science	Enzyme Process
Cytoplan	Advanced Nutrition	Beres	Standard Process
Nutriscene	Health Body Products	Arophar	Dr Donsbach Jason Winter

The most comprehensive stockist of vitamin and nutritional supplements, homoeopathic and biochemic remedies, herbal and Ayurvedic products and special diets

Healthcraft	Kordel	Seven Seas	Celaton
Lanes	Bioceuticals	Ortis	Floradix
Fsc	Meadowcroft	Comvita	Seatone
Power	Biohealth	Kwar	Wassen
Am Nutrition	Healthlife	Hofels	Lifeplan
Regina	Effamol	Pure-Gar	
Bio force	Newera	Wala	Swedish Bitters
Potters	Weleda	Salus-Haus	Health & Heather
Gerards	Khan Marigold	Arkopharma	Herbs of Grace
Bach	Ayurvedic Co.	Biostrath	Dried Herbs
Nelsons	of Great Britain	Obbekipharm	Planetary Formulas
Ainsworth			Specialists
Kan Herbals	East-West Herbs	Pascoe	Herbal Supplies

SPECIALIST PRODUCTS

Green Magma	Superdophilus	Algivit	Aloe Vera juice
Chlorella	Primedophillus	Colon	Argille clay
Guarana	Pfaffia	Cleansing kits	Seavit
Imedeen	Kervrans Silica	Elagen	Viracin
Tanalbit	Blue-Green Algae	Tea-Tree Press.	Tree Syrup

SPECIALIST SKINCARE COSMETICS

Ying Yang	Rachael Perry	Blackmores	Annemarie Borlind
Austrian Moor	Millcreek	Tonialg	Aromatherapy Oils
Weleda	Pierre Cattier	Antica	Dead Sea Products
Tisserand	Bodytreats	Gerards	Kneipp

EXTENSIVE RANGE OF HEALTH BOOKS

LIBRARY/BOOKSHOP/EDUCATION CENTRE

The Centre incorporates a Library/Bookshop with an extensive selection of books, not only on health and nutrition but also on the whole range of alternative and complementary therapies, self development and psychology, and new age. With no obligation to buy, clients are encouraged to browse – there are plenty of leaflets around advertising courses and seminars relating to lifestyle and health. The Centre is uniquely placed to make a positive contribution to education

Books/Information on:

Alternative Therapies: Aromatherapy & Massage, Acupuncture, Alexander Technique, Bach Flower Therapy, Crystal Therapy, Chiropractic, Homoeopathy, Iridology, Kinesiology, Osteopathy, Reflexology, Shiatshu, Spiritual Healing, Tibetan medicine.

Natural Health: Ailments, Allergies, Fitness, Slimming Beauty, Food combining, General good health, Healthy NON-Vegetarian cook books, Herbs & Herbal Medicine, Macrobiotics.

Natural food healing, Nutrition, Parents & Childcare, Special Diets, Vegetarianism, Vitamins & Minerals, Women's Health, Environment, Green Issues.

Self Development & Psychology: Positive thinking, Recovery, Motivation and Self Improvement.

New age: General New Age, Yoga & Meditation.

HOW TO FIND US

The Centre is located on the lower ground floor, being served by a lift for easy access by disabled visitors.

OPENING TIMES:
Mon - Fri 9am-7pm
Weekend hrs: Please phone for further information.

OPEN TO GENERAL PUBLIC

MAIL ORDER HOTLINE: 071 - 436 5122 / 071- 631 0156
☆ ALL MAJOR CREDIT CARDS ACCEPTED FOR PAYMENT
☆ ORDERS PLACED BY NOON DISPATCHED SAME DAY

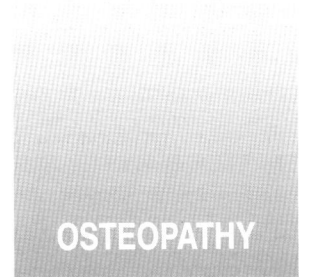

OSTEOPATHY

Osteopathy is one of the most widely used of all complementary medicines and although it is not readily available on the National Health Service, more and more general practitioners will refer patients to osteopaths.

Osteopathy aims to diagnose and treat mechanical problems in the body's framework of bones, joints, muscles and ligaments, which may be caused by injury, stress or general wear and tear.

People with spinal problems such as low back pain and neck pain account for more than half of an osteopath's workload. They can also bring relief to sufferers from stress and work related problems in other parts of the body.

Sportspeople with injuries to muscles or joints and older people feeling the onset of osteoarthritis can benefit from osteopathy, as can pregnant women suffering from the posture changes of their extra weight load.

The osteopath will take a detailed record of symptoms and a full medical history at a first consultation and will carry out a detailed physical examination of the patient sitting, standing, lying down and performing certain movements. Treatment sessions last about 30 minutes and will include gentle massage to release taut muscles as well as the more dynamic manipulation traditionally associated with osteopathy. The rapid movement of a fixed or restricted joint through its full range of movement can result in a rapid improvement in acute conditions but the number of sessiones needed for successful treatment varies with the condition.

Cranial manipulation has become increasingly common recently and can relieve head and facial pain.

For further help contact:
The General Council and Register of Osteoparths
56 London Street, Reading
Berks RG1 4SQ
Tel: 0734 576585

Cranial Osteopathic Association
478 Baker Street, Enfield, Middlesex EN1 3QS
Annual Basic Training Courses and Advanced Training Courses, 3 day conference and 1 day seminar
Telephone: 081 367 5561

Complementary Medicine Centre 9 Corporation Street, Taunton, Somerset TA1 4AJ
Tel: 0823 325022

The Nutri Centre
7 Park Crescent
London W1N 3HE
Tel: 071 436 5122
Fax: 071 436 5171

Mrs N Manston MNIMH MRO (Member of Registered of Osteopaths) 5 Church Street, Beckley, Oxon OX3 9UT Tel: 0865 735 784

H Simpson, DO NCSO, MGO(Lon), MICAK, MRSH, MHPA, MAA, MCKORE Merseyside Tel: 0744 883737

Derek Law MD (MA) DO MBEDA MGO MRH
Stoke Prior, 25 Poole Road, Westbourne, Bournemouth, Dorset
Tel: 0202 764161

Rex Thurstan DMO M PhyA MBEOA
The Cottage Clinic,
25 Sea Road, Bexhill-on-Sea, Sussex
Tel: 0424 222070

Mr Rupert Chapman DO(Hons) MRO
43 A Warwick Way,
London SW1V 1QS
Tel: 071 834 0861

OZONE THERAPY

Ozone has a long pedigree in industry with water purification as its widest application. It is an effective antiviral, antifungal and antimicrobial agent, and although widely used in Germany and Austria, it is still hardly known in the UK.

The range of conditions for which this treatment is used is wide and includes acute and chronic viral conditions, badly healing wounds or ulcers and conditions where there is oxygen depletion in the tissues, such as angina or peripheral blood vessel disase.

Ozone therapy's oxygen generating effect has been shown to have immune-stimulating and anti-flammatory properties in chronic inflammatory conditions of the bowel and joints. It can also be used with nutritional therapies for heart disease and other conditions.

For further help contact:
Dr F Schellander
Liongate Clinic, 8 Chilston Rd,
Tunbrldge Wells,
Kent TN4 9LT
Tel: 0892 543535

POLARITY THERAPY

Polarity Therapy is a very effective form of treatment which is much sought after in this age of holistic and complementary approaches to ill health Developed by Dr Randolph Stone DO DC ND, it employs a profound system that blends Eastern and Western concepts of health. It deals with the whole person – mentally, emotionally and physically – by helping the body to heal itself naturally.

There are trained polarity therapists in Great Britain and Ireland, Europe, USA, Canada, Australia and South Africa.

Polarity therapy works on many different levels: subtle energy, nervous, musculoskeletal, heart, lungs, digestive systems, gynaeco-

---

Liongate Clinic

8 Chilston Road, Tunbridge Wells, Kent TN4 9LT
Telephone: 0892 543535

A *holistic private medical clinic offering*
CHELATION THERAPY and OZONE THERAPY for HEART DISEASE, ARTERIOSCLEROSIS and related conditions

Also at:
Newport, Shropshire 0952 813219
Eastbourne, East Sussex - 0323 734664

Re • Vision

Centre for Integrative Psychosynthesis
● Three year Diploma course intergrating different therapeutic schools for a holistic approach to counselling and therapy
● Introductory one week courses
● Weekend self-development courses

8 Chatsworth Road, London NW2 4BN
Tel No: 081 451 2165

logical (excellent in pregnancy and after-care) and at emotional and mental levels. It has been found useful in dealing with many varied and different expressions of disease by unlocking the holding patterns that create the symptoms.

A trained registered polarity therapist (RPT) can incorporate four aspects of PT: In **Bodywork** the therapist uses a series of subtle penetrative manipulations with their hands. This can be relaxing and restorative and can allow emotional and personal issues to surface and become clearer. In **Awareness Skills** the therapist is trained to allow the body and mind relationship to seek a fuller and deeper interaction. **Health Building** and/or **Cleansing Diets** and procedures help detoxify the system, freeing up life giving energy. Each person is assessed individually as no one procedure is correct for everyone. **Polarity Stretching Exercises** release stagnation and allow the client to continue and maintain their healing process

The combination of these four aspects of polarity therapy allows a person to take responsibility for their own well-being.

With the client's permission where appropriate, the therapist will liaise with his or her GP.

Last, but not least the polarity therapist is trained to treat their client with kindness and understanding together with a deep care for their well-being. .

The Polarity Therapy Association UK is a member of the British Polarity Council and the British Complementary Medicine Association (BCMA) and the Institute for Complementary Medicine.

For further help contact:
The Polarity Therapy Association UK
Association Secretary
Tel: 0373 452250

The Polarity Education Trust runs introductory seminar days, foundation courses and full professional training. For details call 0373 452250

THE POLARITY THERAPY ASSOCIATION UK

Registered polarity therapists are available throughout Britain. For other therapists and areas not listed please contact the Secretary on 0373 452250

S Barton	Sussex area	Tel: 0273 689215	D Haas	Surrey & Berks area	Tel: 0483 423352
I Comboy	Devon area	Tel: 0364 42143	K Hughes	London S & W	Tel: 081 769 1126
H Cooley	London SW area	Tel: 081 473 1452	M Jenkins	North London	Tel: 081 888 6982
J Cooley	London E&SW area	Tel: 081 874 0513	E MacDonald	Surrey & London S&W	Tel: 081 942 3781
C Devereux	Hampshire area	Tel: 0590 645055	A Mitchell	Dorset area	Tel: 0963 220522
S Delfont	Devon area	Tel: 0364 652 895	L Newman	Kent and London area	Tel: 0322 348514
A Devin	N London, Middx, Surrey	Tel: 0895 673381	V Pearce	Dorset area	Tel: 0929 553672
J Dann	Midlands area	Tel: 0203 670847	A Roden	Middlesex area	Tel: 081 866 5944
B Dann	Midlands area	Tel: 0203 670847	Alan Russell	Kent and Londonarea	Tel: 081 659 4638
A Doorley	West London area	Tel: 071 602 6210	C Rudd	Norfolk area	Tel: 0263 732523
S DiSabatino	W Yorks area	Tel: 0943 830989	C Squire	W Yorks area	Tel: 0532 782953
A Englehart	Sussex area	Tel: 0273 857303	E Van Vessem		
H Franks	Middlesex area	Tel: 0895 673381		Edinburgh area	Tel: 031 551 5091
A Furnival	S Yorks area	Tel: 0742 586290	F Wright	London WC2, EC3 & NW3	Tel: 071 435 4842
K Farvis	Edinburgh area	Tel: 031 447 5572	D Wilson	Sussex area	Tel: 0273 207316
P Guest	Avon, Somerset, Surrey	Tel: 0373 452250			

PSYCHIC COUNSELLING

A psychic/spiritual counsellor uses a variety of tools to assist their natural capacity to gain information and guidance in problem areas.

A psychic/spiritual counsellor – with the help of their natural abilities – will be able to direct a client to perceive where the condition stems from and to help them in using their new understanding to turn around the process leading to wholeness.

The consultant members of the British Astrological & Pyschic Society have all been stringently vetted within their specific fields. The society was founded in 1976 by Russell Grant.

For further help contact:
British Astrological and Psychic Society
124 Trefoil Crescent,
Broadfield, Crawley,
W. Sussex RH11 9EZ

Temple
Psychic Counsellor RMAPC
Healing, including animals
Workshops on psychic awareness
On sale – crystal, minerals gemstones, pendulums, jewellery etc
Tel: 081 367 1495

PSYCHOTHERAPY

People usually seek psychotherapy at times of crisis or change in their lives. They can talk through a problem in a more structured way than talking to a sympathetic friend or a non-specific counsellor.

A psychotherapy session can cover many topics including experiences, feelings and attitudes to others. It can involve anger, sadness, disagreement, advice and encouragement, but the psychotherapist's professional training will ensure that each session is structured so the patient benefits.

The psychotherapist is providing a context in which to explore personal issues and feelings in a non-judgmental relationship. A session usually lasts about 50 minutes. A person may stay with psychotherapy on a weekly basis over several years but shorter-term therapy can help immediate problems.

Psychotherapists, unlike psychiatrists, do not prescribe drug or shock therapy treatments. They can help anyone with relationship or behavioural problems, those with phobias, sufferers from depression, tension and stress. Psychotherapy may also help in the treatment of physical ailments related to emotional problems.

For further help contact:
National Association of Counsellors, Hypnotherapists and Psychotherapists
145 Coleridge Road
Cambridge CB1 3PN

Re-Vision Centre for Integrative Psychosynthesis
8 Chatsworth Road,
London NW2 4BN
Tel: 081 451 2165
See ad page 54

Complementary Medicine Centre, 9, Corporation Street,
Taunton, Somerset TA1 4AJ
Tel: 0823 325022

Alison Perrott SP DipA,
MISPA, MISMA, MASK, MTMI,
The SEED Institute,
10 Magnolia Way, Fleet,
Hants, GU1 9JZ
Tel: 0252 626448
See ad under Courses

Maggie Naish Cert in Counselling, Member BAC
RGN Natural Choice Therapy Centre 24 St John Street,
Ashbourne, Derbys DE6 1GH
Tel: 0335 346096

The Springfield Clinic of Natural Healing
Springfield House, Newgate,
Wilmslow, Cheshire
SK9 5LL.
Healing with a difference.
Tel: 0625 523155

The National College
12 Cross Street, Nelson,
Lancs BB9 7EN
Tel: 0282 699378

RADIANCE TECHNIQUE

The Radiance Technique® is a transcendental energy science, a meditation with the hands. The seven degrees of the authentic system were rediscovered from Tibetan Sanscrit sutras in the last century and now provide a highly effective method for relaxing, calming, revitalising and energising.

Benefiting every level of the body-mind-spirit dynamic, it promotes personal development, healing/wholing and pursuit of the highest goals. It is a simple hands-on system which may be learned by young and old, and can easily be used on a daily basis.

TRT can be taught in a professional seminar from an accredited teacher or you can receive sessions from a transcendental practitioner.

For further help contact:

Ingrld St Clare
The Radlance Technlque®
Semlnars
8 Furnace Lane, Flnedon
Northamptonshire NN9 5NZ
Tel: 0536 725292

REBIRTHING

Rebirthing works with the idea that your life is a perfect reflection of your thoughts, and that all you need to have your life work the way you want it, is within you.

Negative thinking about ourselves and life can create patterns of tension in the body, mind and emotions. The natural breathing rhythm used in rebirthing unravels and gently opens up old stuck areas and brings them back to life.

As the client starts to re-experience the old patterns, they have the chance to realise the power they have in shaping the way they think and react to situations. With that realisation comes the chance to transform relationships with friends, family, body, work, money, and most importantly, with yourself.

For further help contact:

British Rebirth Society
5 Manor Road,
Cotcott, Bridgewater,
Somerset

Sue Lawson
"Breathe and maximise your potential for living"
Tel: 071 372 6031

REFLEXOLOGY

The ancient healing art of reflexology has been known to man for thousands of years. It is based on the concept that every part of the body is connected by energy pathways which terminate in the reflex areas on the feet and hands. Reflexology is the practice of working on these reflexes to produce a reaction and relaxation in the corresponding body areas. By applying controlled pressure to the reflex areas on the feet, the body is stimulated to achieve its own state of equilibrium and good health.

Due to stress, illness or poor lifestyle, the energy pathways of the body may become blocked or congested preventing the body from working at peak efficiency. The sensitive, trained hands of a qualified reflexologist can detect tiny deposits and tensions in the feet which block the vital energy pathways. By releasing these tiny obstructions, toxins are eliminated and the circulation improved, restoring the free flow of energy and nutrients to the body's cells. This gentle therapy encourages the body to heal itself

at its own pace, often counteracting a lifetime of misuse. When choosing a reflexologist, it is wise to ensure that the therapist has been properly trained, works to a professional code of ethics and is fully insured to practise on the public.
For further help contact:
The Association of Relexologists
27 Old Gloucester Street,
London WC1 3XX
Tel: 0273 771061

British School of Reflexology
92 Sheering Road,
Old Harlow Essex
Tel: 0279 429060

The Edinburgh School of Natural Therapy,
2 London Street EH3 6NA
Tel: 031 557 3901

Rosemary Ryan
Registered Practioner of the Ingham Method
Ilford, Essex
Tel: 081 551 8179

Complementary Medicine Centre, 9 Corporation Street,
Taunton, Somerset TA1 4AJ
Tel: 0823 325022

Enrico Dodson, 21 Cowlersley Lane, Cowlersley,
Huddersfield HP4 5TY Tel: 0484 641982

Alison Mold BEd (Hons) Dip BWY (Cert in Remedial Yoga) Dip SPA ISPA
Natural Choice Centre
24 St John Street, Ashbourne,
Derbyshire DE6 1GH
Tel: 0335 346096

Salon Elysee Hair & Beauty, Cumbria
Comprehensive range of treatments available in relaxing surroundings to reduce stress and revitalise energy.
Reflexologist
Elizabeth A Weir MAR MIFA
Tel: 0228 28222

Reflexology Practitioner. Certified course, Accredited course with Reflexologists Society. BCMA & ICM Registers. Workshop venues. Cheltenham Hoths
School of Reflexology,
39 Prestbury Road,
Cheltenham GL52 2PI
Tel: 0242 512601

Manchester School of Massage
MSM

✣ **INTRODUCTORY & DIPLOMA COURSES** ✣
MASSAGE AROMATHERAPY REFLEXOLOGY SPORTS THERAPY ON SITE MASSAGE SHIATSU

77 RUSSELL ROAD MANCHESTER M16 8AR
TEL: 061 862 9752

For sports injuries, back, neck and arms, leg, joint and muscle pains. Better health for mind and body
Contact:
Enrico Dodson LCSP (Assoc), MIIR, MBSAM
21 Cowlersley Lane, Huddersfield HD4 5TY
Tel: 0484 641982

REFLEXOLOGIST
Registered Practioner of the Ingham Method
Reduced rates for OAPs and UB40s
Ilford, Essex
Tel: 081 551 8179

The British School of Reflexology
PRINCIPAL Ann Gillanders MBSR,MBSA

TRAIN TO BE A REFLEXOLOGY PRACTITIONER THROUGH THE MOST PROFESSIONAL ORGANISATION.

ANN GILLANDERS HAS BEEN INVOLVED IN TEACHING, PRACTISING AND PROMOTING REFLEXOLOGY INTERNATIONALLY FOR 17 YEARS AND HAS A WEALTH OF KNOWLEDGE TO IMPART

THE SCHOOL HAS EXPANDED VENUES NOW TO INCLUDE

LONDON HARLOW NOTTINGHAM HARROGATE BRISTOL

OUR FOUR PART TRAINING COURSES ARE COMBINED WITH CORRESPONDENCE STUDY. THE COURSE PREPARES PRACTITIONERS FOR ENTRY INTO THE BRITISH REGISTER NOW FORMED

A LIST OF REGISTERED REFLEXOLOGISTS IN YOUR AREA MAY BE OBTAINED BY SENDING A SAE(9X5)

FOR DETAILS OF TRAINING SEND A 40P STAMP FOR A FULL BROCHURE TO:
BRITISH SCHOOL OF REFLEXOLOGY
92 SHEERING ROAD,
OLD HARLOW, ESSEX
TEL 0279 429060

Meg Reid MA MANM
Reflexologist and Reiki
Healer. Clinic at The Trinity
Centre, 21 Trinity Street,
Colchester, Essex.
Home visits also available
To find out how reflexology
can help you reduce stress,
revitalise energy, relieve
illness or act as a preventative therapy call me on
0206 823723

Mrs Margaret Weeds MIFA
MBSR SPA Dip MIPTI ITEC
17 Freckenham Road,
Worlington, Nr Mildenhall,
Suffolk IP28 8SQ
Tel: 0638 716759

Mrs Jones
23 Mellor Road,
Cheadlehume, Stockport
Cheshire
Tel: 061 485 4009

Mrs Dawson
Reflexology, Holistic
Massage and Hypnotherapy
Loughton, Essex
Tel: 081 508 2553

Rachel Stanford LCSP (Assoc)
IPII
The Guildhall Treatment
Room, 55 Church Street, Eye
Suffolk IP23 7BD
Tel: 0379 870 938

Mrs Naomi Shepherd
MAR ITEC
Penfold Lodge Road, Hurst,
Reading, Berks RG10 0EG
Tel: 0734 340755
also at Natural Therapy
Clinic, 2 Boyne Valley Road
Maidenhead Berks SL6 4ED
Tel: 0628 72005

York Reflexology Centre,
22A Fishergate York YO1 4AB
Tel: 0904 651544 or 422149

Cristina Weiland MAR AHAF
Sun Cottage, 69 Terrace
Road, Walton on Thames,
Surrey KT12 2SW
Tel: 0932 247887

Manchester School of
Massage
77 Russell Road,
Manchester M16 8AR
Tel 061 862 9752

REGRESSION THERAPY

Change comes when we can step back and consider the greater perspective. Regression is a safe way to do that. It is not simply a process through which one catches glimpses of past lives. It is seen as an expansion of consciousness into timelessness.

In a comfortably relaxed state, normally the result of creative visualisation, the client is given the opportunity to 'step out of present time' into a safe place – a state of 'all being' – to connect with all the multi-dimensions of being and bring them into alignment.

From that state of trust, they can observe and release the attachments and beliefs that have acted like magnets to draw them into the same situations, reactions and behaviour patterns, possibly lifetime after lifetime. The release of those seeming limitations makes space for hidden potential to come to the surface and

---

REFLEXOLOGY
The whole body treatment carried out on the feet by massage.
Home visits carried out in Harrogate, Wetherby, and York.
For further information and appointments ring
Ian Sawkins MAR on York **0904 651544** or **422149**
York Reflexology Centre
22A Fishergate, York YO1 4AB

REGRESSION FOR ALIGNMENT
TRANSFORMATION AND WHOLENESS
with KATHRYN PLAYER
INDIVIDUAL SESSIONS, LECTURES AND WORKSHOPS AND 2 TAPE SET
"REGRESSION - A REMEMBERING OF PAST LIVES"
TEL: 071 582 4061 (11AM/4.30PM) FOR DETAILS & ACCESS/VISA ORDERS.
REGRESSION TAPE SET £19.99 + 75P P&P.
Cheques to Illimitable Productions, Robinson Barber & Co, COnnOp House,
517 Hertford Road, Enfield, Middlesex EN3 5UA

gives access to memory-experiences of times of fulfilment, abundance and love, so the whole energy field becomes those resonances, drawing to it a full and abundant reality that reflects those quality experiencies back in sympathetic response to the eliminations of electro-magnetic patterns.

You literally become what you apparently lacked and, therefore, achieve wholeness.

For further help contact:
Kathryn Player
Regressionist, ITEC,
Healer Member of the National Federation of Spiritual Healers,
c/o Robinson Barber & Co.
Connop House,
517 Hertford Road, Enfield,
Middx EN3 5UA
Tel: 071 582 4061
(11am-4.30pm)

REIKI

Reiki is a gentle, simple healing art, rediscoverd in Japan at the turn of the century by Dr Mikao Usui. The word 'Reiki' means Universal Life Energy and this energy is transferred to the person receiving treatment through the practitioner's hands.

The client lies, or sits if lying is difficult, comfortably while the practitioner places his or her hands lightly on the body in a sequence of pre-determined positions. These positions can be varied if there is a specific need.

There is no need for the removal of any clothing and one treatment will generally last 60 to 90 minutes.

Most people experience the treatment as warming, soothing and relaxing, bringing a feeling of well-being and peace mind. They may also experience heat from the practitioner's hands. The vital energy of Reiki stimulates the body's own ability to heal itself. It works quickly for acute problems and will help chronic problems, given time. Reiki can heal the body, mind and spirit.

For further help contact:
The Reiki Association
8 Ashmore Road,
Cotteridge,
Birmingham B30 2HA
Tel: 021 433 3212

Pamela Hollis AERP
Violet Hill Studio, Centre for Creative Healing, 6 Violet Hill,
St John's Wood,
London NW8 9EB
Tel: 071 586 5864
Violet Hill Studios
tel: 071 624 6101

Meg Reid MA MANM
Clinic at The Trinity Centre,
21 Trinity Street, Colchester,
Essex.
Tel: 0206 823723

Andrea Lock
Counselling, Reiki Healing, Rebirthing
Stowmarket, Suffolk
For appointments
tel: 0449 774869

ROLFING

Rolfing is a method of structural integration and alignment of the body developed by American biochemist Ida Rolf (1896-1979) who saw that the body's posture and muscular tensions were held in place by the sinewy web of connective tissue. These take their shape in response to injuries and traumas we have suffered, habits we have adopted and the ever present force of gravity.

The Rolfing practitioner works gently with the hands, untangling the web of connective tissue. The client assists by making slow precise movement, stretching and opening the tissue. Sometimes this can be momentarily uncomfortable; for others, deep emotional release can occur during the session. The Rolfer and client work together to build the trust necessary to sustain these changes. Gradually over a series of ten sessions, posture improves, muscles reset their tone, and the body acquires a lightness and responsiveness in carriage and movement.

Improving the posture can help combat chronic fatigue, joint, muscle and back pain and aid the function of the internal organs. Rolfing is also useful in resolving unfinished emotional issues which are dramatised in the postural attitudes and chronic holding patterns of the body.

All certified Rolfers are trained by the Rolf Institute in Boulder, Colorado, USA.

For further help contact:

Jennie Crewdson
Certified Rolfer
London SW1V 2DR
Tel: 071 834 1493

Anna Orren
Certified Rolfer, Bristol
Tel: 0272 264917

SHAMANISM

The pollution of air and water, toxic waste buried in the earth and the sea, nuclear radiation leaks, demolition of the rainforests, reduction in the protective ozone layer and other environmental disasters have led many people to question modern lifestyles. At a deep level each of us knows that it cannot go on, yet we do not know how to turn the tide.

The teachings of the ancient shamanic cultures, who for thousands of years lived successfully in harmony and balance with the earth and plant and animal kingdoms, are once again coming to the fore.

Contemporary shamanism is the adaptation of the ancient teachings to help

---

ROLFING

uses hands and elbows with controlled pressure and direction to release patterns of tension that run through the body. Rolfer and client work together to realign physical structure towards a level of deeper relaxation, heightened energy and greater wellbeing.
Now offered in Bristol by
ANNA ORREN, Certified Rolfer
Tel: 0272 264917

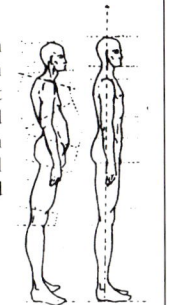

THE
ROLFING
METHOD OF STRUCTURAL INTEGRATION
- Is a method of deep tissue massage which manipulates the body's connective tissue (fascia).
- Improving the body's relationship with gravity
- Easing back, neck and joint pain
- Helping resolve unfinished emotional issues which are dramatised in postural attitudes of the body
- Improve posture, creating more energy
- Making you look and feel better

For further information please contact Jennie Crewdson, Certified Rolfer on 071 834 1493

urban, suburban and all people of today to create a way of life that is sustainable.

Shamanism is not about beliefs – in fact, it is not a belief system at all. It is a path to knowledge which is gained through experience of life, through ceremonies, rituals, prayer and meditation, drumming, singing, dancing, celebrating and through trials and tests.

Knowledge is something that works, that stands up to test, that is known from the inside, unlike belief which is something taken on from outside, from others. Wars are fought over beliefs, never over knowledge.

Shamanism is a practical, non-dogmatic pyscho-spiritual path which leads the seeker to the place of inner knowledge and enables him to walk in balance and touch the world with beauty in the great vision quest called life.

For further help contact:
Eagle's Wing Centre for Contemporary Shamanism
58 Westbere Road,
London NW2 3RU
Tel: 071 435 8174

SHIATUS

Shiatsu, Japanese 'finger pressure' therapy is a natural healing discipline, springing from the same ancient principles as acupuncture. Like acupuncture, Shiatsu works by rebalancing the body's vital energy flow in order to promote good health and treat specific problems. However, in Shiatsu, the practitioner uses thumbs and fingers, elbows and even knees to apply pressure and stretching to the energy lines known as meridians or channels.

It allows the receiver to relax deeply and get in touch with his/her body's own healing abilities. Treatment usually leaves a feeling of calmness and well-being, of being more in touch with one's body and self.

Shiatsu affects all levels of our being - the physical, emotional, psychological and spiritual. Treatment is attuned to the individual's personal development of total health and character. Advice may be given on diet, exercise and lifestyle, encouraging self understanding and greater independence in health matters.

For further help contact:
The European Shiatsu School
Dept AC, ESS Central Adminstration, High Banks, Lockeridge, Nr Marlborough, Wiltshire SN8 4EQ
Tel: 0672 86362

The Devon School of Shiatsu
The Coach House,
Buckyette Farm,
Littlehempston, Totnes,
Devon TQ9 6ND
Tel: 0803 762593

The British School of Shiatsu-Do (Maidstone)
Ken Oliver MRSS
Clinics in Maidstone, Rochester and Gravesend
For details of treatments and courses telephone:
0622 750605 (day)
0622 820397 (evenings/weekends)

The Shiatsu College London
Unit 62, 126-8 Barlby Road,
London W10
Tel: 081 964 1449

Vivienne de Jacolyn
MRSS ITEC
Home meets for women only.
Tel: 071 624 8616

Mike Craske BSc DIC PhD
Dip in Shiatsu and oriental medicine,
Natural Choice Therapy Centre, 24 St John Street,
Ashbourne, Derbys DE6 1GH
Tel: 0335 346096

The Ki Kai Shiatsu Centre
172A Arlington Road,
Camden, London NW1
Tel: 081 368 9050

The EUROPEAN SHIATSU SCHOOL

Branches:
LONDON
BATH
BELFAST
BIRMINGHAM
BOURNEMOUTH
BRIGHTON
BRISTOL
CANTERBURY
CARDIFF
CUMBRIA
FRANCE
MALVERN
MARLBOROUGH
OXFORD
READING
SOUTHAMPTON
STOKE-ON-TRENT
TIVERTON
GREECE
SPAIN
Plus many more pending...

FOR DETAILS/PROSPECTUS
PLEASE SEND 3 x 1st class stamps.
Dept AC
ESS Central Adminstration,
High Banks, Lockeridge, Nr Marlborough,
Wiltshire SN8 4EQ
Tel: 0672 86362

THE MOST WIDELY NETWORKED TRAINING ESTABLISHMENT FOR BODYWORK THERAPY IN THE UK & EUROPE

SHIATSU
VIVIENNE DE JACOLYN MRSS ITEC
Shiatsu relieves stress, restores vitality. Advice on diet and exercises. Home meets for women only. Please telephone for an appointment
071 624 8616

EAGLE'S WING
Centre for Contemporary Shamanism
LEO RUTHERFORD AND FRIENDS
Based on the medicine wheel teachings and the ancient wisdom of those who live close to the earth.
Courses from a day to a year long.
Programme/info: Eagle's Wing, 58 Westbere Road, London NW2 3RU Tel: 071 435 8174

The Devon School of Shiatsu
- Regular Introductory Classes
- 1 Year Foundation Course
- 3 Year Practitioner Training Course
- Practice and Clinic Days
- In own rooms in Devonshire countryside

Full programme from:
The Devon School of Shiatsu
The Coach House, Buckyette Fram,
Littlehempston, Totnes,
Devon TQ9 6ND
Tel: 0803 762593

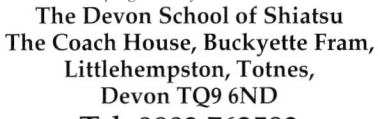

SHIATSU TRAINING

The Ki Kai Shiatsu Centre offers individual treatments, introductory classes and professional diploma courses.

For details and enquiries write to:

THE KI KAI SHIATSU CENTRE
172A Arlington Road,
Camden, London NW1
Telephone: 081 368 9050

SHIATSU (continued)

Josephine Pridmore
MRSST SHIATSU - Japanese healing therapy. Dorset.
Josephine is a qualified practitioner and teacher of Shiatsu and Yoga.
For further information please telephone
0202 739868 or
(Mobile 0850 477287)

Complementary Medicine Centre, 9 Corporation Street, Taunton, Somerset TA1 4AJ
Tel: 0823 325022

John Tidder MRSS
Shiatsu Practitioner
Registered with The Shiatsu Society
114 Glebe Road, Norwich
NR2 3QJ
For appointments tel:
0603 626153

Lavender House Aromatherapy and Shiatsu Centre, 30/31 Henley Sreet, Stratford-upon-Avon
Tel: 0789 204775

Sarah Wale B Sc (Hons)
MRSS, Wisteria House,
Blunham, Bedfordshire
Tel: Biggleswade 0767 40236

SPIRITUAL DEVELOPMENT AND HEALING

Spiritual healing is the channelling of healing energies through the healer to the patient. It re-energises and relaxes the patients to enable their own natural resources to deal with illness or injury. By 'attunement' – perhaps best described as a combination of empathy and intent – either in the presence of the patient or at a distance, and by directing energy, usually through the hands, the healer seeks to supplement the depleted energy of the recipient, dealing with stress at whatever level it exists and releasing the body's own recuperative abilities to deal with the problem in the most effective way for that individual.

Patients receiving healing tend to experience sensations of being re-energised or relaxed, 'pins and needles', heat or coolness, and pain coming to the surface and dispersing, indicating that the energies are indeed going to work. Healing can be given for any illness, stress or injury as a therapy which is completely natural, has no side effects and is complementary to any other therapy.

It can be helpful in a wide range of physical and psychological conditions. The medically diagnosed nature of the illness appears to be irrelevant to the outcome and case histories range from the trivial to the terminal in which healing seems to have made an important, perhaps even overriding, contribution to recovery.

Aside from its value in relieving pain and restoring function, healing is also notable for initiating improvements in patients' attitudes and clarity of thought, and in their quality of life.

GENUINE SPIRITUAL
A real and personal; answer to ANY PROBLEM
Just send £10 stating need for
PERSONALLY PROGRAMMED CRYSTAL
in velvet pouch to : **Spiritual Crystals, 3 Rhiwbank Avenue, Colwyn Bay LL29 7PH Tel: (0492) 531220**

RELAXATION & SELF-HEALING
WITH KATE WILLIAMS
Follow Kate's voice to gently unwind and find a source of energy and peace within. £7.50 inc p&p. For full details and order form RING 081 8887927

Clearing negative thought patterns. Cutting the ties that bind. Clearing physical and emotional energy blocks. Looking at relationships and their Karmic connection.
Sharon Jarvis works with individuals and groups, helping them improve the way they communicate and perceive life's lessons

Sharon Jarvis
3 Thornwood, Mile End, Colchester
Essex CO4 5LR Tel: 0206 854407

For further help contact:
National Federation of Spiritual Healers
Old Manor Farm Studio,
Church Street,
Sunbury-on-Thames,
Middx TW16 6RG
Tel: 0932 783164

Spritual Crystals
3 Rhiwbank Avenue,
Colwyn Bay LL29 7PH
Tel: 0492 531250

Distance or contact healing
Barbara Lewis
28 Erwgoch, Waun Fawr,
Aberystwyth,
Dyfed SY23 3AZ
Tel: 0970 623040

Sharon Jarvis
3 Thornwood, Mile End,
Colchester, Essex CO4 5LR
Tel: 0206 854407

Sarah Wale
B Sc (Hons) MRSS

Registered Shiatsu Practitioner

Wisteria House,
Blunham, Bedfordshire
Tel: Biggleswade
0767 40236

STRESS MANAGEMENT

Anything that is a threat to bodily health or which adversely affects the body's normal functioning system can be termed as stress. Stress can come in many forms but generally it is either good, bad or ugly. There are a variety of skills which enable us to make the most of good stress, keep bad stress under control and to avoid, or recover from the effects of ugly stress. We can also learn to have more control over mind and body.

Stress is not a disease and stress management is not a form of therapy. The skills can be used to enhance the effectiveness of any therapy, as well as for personal and organisational development.

For further help contact:
Dr Paul Scarrow B Med Sci
BM BS, Medi Scene Health Care, Notts
Tel/Fax: 0777 708060
See ads under Biofeedback, Healthy Living and Muscle Learning Therapy

Alison Perrott SP DipA,
MISPA, MISMA, MASK, MTMI,
The SEED Insitute, 10
Magnolia Way, Fleet, Hants
GU13 9JZ Tel: 0252 626448
See ad under Courses

TAPE RELAXATION

Listening to music is a passive form of relaxation and one of the most effective ways of combating stress, releasing mental tension and preventing illness. Today, one can choose from an enormous range of relaxation tapes - mostly from New Age shops - that will help to calm the mind and body from the pressures of everyday life.

In this relaxed state, there is regular diaphragmatic breathing, muscular relaxation and mental calmness. The body uses less energy than it normally and there is less work for the major organs.

Regular tape relaxation excercises have been shown to lower blood pressure and improve all-round performance.

For further help contact:
Kate Williams
Tel: 081 8887927

YOGA

Yoga has for centuries provided a system of physical and mental disciplines to improve strength, stamina and flexibility while calming the mind and relieving stress.

Students attending their first class often report a surprising sense of wellbeing, when they had expected to feel tired and stiff.

The British Medical Association describes yoga as a complementary self-help therapy. Being complementary, yoga can be practised together with orthodox medicine and it provides a basis on which the individual can raise resistance to ill health.

This makes it very different from other approaches, for the yoga practitioner shares with the patient, realising that one must practise what one preaches. In recent years it has been recognised increasingly that the yoga approach can produce invaluable help in a whole range of chronic problems and disabilities.

While yoga is widely known for its physical component - the asana, or posture - its core is a whole series of approaches leading to calming the mind and creating a greater state of positivity.

For further help contact:
Yoga For Health Foundation
Ickwell Bury,
Biggleswade,
Beds. SG18 9EF
Tel: 0767 627271

Surrey Yoga Centre
Church Farm House, Spring Close Lane, Cheam, Surrey SM3 8PU Tel: 081 644 0309

ZEN MEDITATION

Zen meditation is a form of Buddhist meditation which can be one more tool in the battle against stress. It presupposes some knowledge and desire to practise Buddhism on the part of the practitioner. In the initial stages of learning to meditate the purpose is to still the mind. The techniques used are the same in most Buddhist schools and consist of concentrating on the act of breathing either by counting breaths of by observing each inhalation and exhalation, most usually as they pass the tip of the nose.

For further help contact:
The Buddhist Society
58 Ecclestone Square
London SW1V 1PH

SURREY YOGA CENTRE
Church Farm House,
Spring Close Lane, Cheam,
Surrey SM3 8PU
Tel: 081 644 0309

Yoga meets the present day need to counteract stress.
Weekly classes, residential weekends, practice cassettes

Ruth White 081 644 0309

A HEALTHIER WAY OF LIVING

The desire for a better, healthier standard of living is a perfectly natural one.

Feeling okay may seem enough. But the truth is you could feel far better. Since 1979 The Institute of Optimum Nutrition has been researching the difference between feeling alright, and feeling totally healthy. A patient once described health as 'blissfully oblivious of myself all day long'. In other words, at ease, as opposed to un-ease – or worse – dis-ease.

The Institute of Optimum Nutrition is an independent charity which exists to help people achieve optimum nutrition and reach for the highest level of health. Health is not just an absence of disease, it's an abundance of well being that depends on the food you eat, the environment you live in, your fitness and state of mind.

The massive increase in the sale of nutritional supplements indicates an upsurge of interest in personal health, and foods with a powerful health image are now available in abundance.

Wholegrain cereals and pulses, nuts and seeds, dried fruit and honey can all provide us with a healthy sustained diet.

Naturally, well being can't be achieved overnight. It's a gradual step by step process.

A well balanced diet means a mix of the carbohydrates, fibre, fats, proteins, vitamins and minerals we need to thrive. Not all foods have these, so we should eat a variety of food in the hope we'll get our nutrients.

That's the theory. But everybody is different and it can be difficult to eat a balanced diet unless you know precisely what you need.

Nationwide surveys in the past decade confirm that many people lack the basic recommended levels of nutrients, even though they think they eat a well balanced diet.

Skin problems, lack of energy, frequent colds, aching joints, poor concentration, even depression can all be caused by malnutrition.

More and more people are becoming vegetarians and vegans in Western society, some because of their worries about modern methods of animal farming and others purely on health grounds. Any diet which actually makes you think about what you eat and your lifestyle should be beneficial, but macrobiotics, based on the Chinese philosophy of yin and yang, is almost a complete way of life, involving exercise and environmental considerations as well as diet.

Apart from diet, sensible regular exercise can help the body resist many diseases and disorders. Sleeplessness, digestive troubles, constipation, lethargy after work, accumulating nervous tension can all be worked off by leading a life that includes regular exercise.

Health farms offer a wide range of therapies and treatments usually centred around calorie-controlled diets and fasting.

There are also a number of institutions and centres offering courses designed to lead to a healthier way of life and even to a complete new philosophy.

A number of such courses, health holiday and retreats are listed on pages 68-74.

Medi Scene Health Care
"In the Pursuit of Health and Wellness"

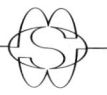

People are now more aware of their own health and wish to be well, but what *are* the ingredients of health and wellnes?

We offer you a comprehensive health and wellness service which addresses these factors and covers your area of concern.

We offer you the opportunity to learn skills, by which you can prevent or change the course of a disorder without the reliance on drugs or surgery.

'A wise man ought to realise that health is his most valuable possession' - Hippocrates

For further information or a brochure contact:-
Medi-Scene Health Care,
Lorelei House, Old Blyth Road, Ranby, Retford,
Notts DN22 8HZ
Telephone & Fax: 0777 708060

100% NATURAL
Over 1000 different herbs
Treats Arthritic, Rheumatic, Mouth, Skin and Internal conditions
Sandy Rodgers ITEC Massage
Grove House, Belchamp Walter, Sudbury CO10 7AR
Tel: 0787 313413

The British School of Shiatsu-Do (Bedford Branch)
is currently teaching Foundation Level courses
For further information contact:
S Wale
Telephone: 0767 40236

DIETARY FOODS
Free from gluten, wheat, soya, maize, lactose, egg or milk. No refined sugar or artificial additives
BREADS, PASTAS, BRAN, EGG REPLACER
For further information contact:
General Designs Ltd (Pastarisa/Ener-G Foods Distributor)
PO Box 38, Kingston, Surrey KT2 7YP
081 336 2323

Psychodynamic Bodywork and Counselling
FULL TRAINING IN FOUR CERTIFICATED MODULES

Psychodynamic Bodywork and Counselling is the basis for body psychotherapy and is a profession in its own right. It is based on the work of Wilhelm Reich regarding life energy and on the further development of his concepts by Gerda Boyesen and others in the field of Biodynamic therapy. The first module is a 10 week, part-time Bio-release massage course which offers ITEC professional qualifications to practise as a Holistic Massage Therapist.
Training venue: London N1

For details contact: Alice Jacobus
The Holistic School of Systems Therapy
Admin Office: 178 High Street, Acton, London W3 9NN
Tel: 081 993 6351

GOOD SCENTS
SCHOOL OF NATURAL THERAPIES

Offers professional diploma courses in Anatomy and Physiology, Massage, Aromatherapy, Reflexology. Additional courses available in Pathology and Acupressure.
We teach small classes at reasonable fees to the highest standards.
RQA, ISPA, VTCT, IHBC, ITEC, and IPTI accredited.
Registered member of the Aromatherapy Organisation Council.

9 CHUTE WAY, HIGH SALVINGTON, WORTHING, WEST SUSSEX BN13 3EA

Tel/Fax 0903 694202

COURSES

Athena Counselling Services
Freepost(BR614) Brighton
BN2 2ZZ, Tel: 0273 697376
Fax: 0273 670181
Therapies, workshops, counselling tapes, healing, books, psychometrics, workshop tape sets

Hypnotherapy Control Board
PO Box 180, Bournemouth
BH3 7YR
Tel: 0202 311191 (24 hrs)

The School of Physical
Therapies Group
For details phone your local school:
Basingstoke 0256 475728
Kingston 081 546 0290

Good Scents School of Natural Therapies
9 Chute Way, High Salvington
Worthing,
W Sussex BN13 3EA
Tel/Fax: 0903 694202

FELLSIDE ALEXANDER SCHOOL offers various courses in the Alexander Technique to the general public as well as full-time professional teaching
Fellside Alexander School
Low Fellside, Kendal,
Cumbria LA9 4NJ
Tel: 0539 733045

The SEED Institute
10, Magnolia Way, Fleet
Hants GU13 9JZ
Tel/Fax: 0252 626448
Workshop
Locations: Hants, Northants, Herts, Leics, Scotland
(others considered for 10+ participants)

Natural Healing Centre
Kathleen Huddlestone,
72 Pasture Road, Goole,
North Humberside DN14 6HE
Tel: 0405 769119

The National Association of Counsellors, Hypnotherapists and Psychotherapists
145 Coleridge Road,
Cambridge CB1 3PN

The School of Homoeopathy
CORRESPONDENCE COURSE
& PRACTITIONER COURSE
Interested in homoeopathy? Join our one year Correspondence Course (Open University style) to thoroughly learn the basic principles. Continue on to our two year part-time course to gain your practitioner's diploma, followed by a post-graduate year for Registered Membership of the Society of Homoeopaths
For full details please send A5 SAE to:
Stuart Gracie, Course Manager (D)
The School of Homoeopathy
Yondercott House, Uffculme,
Devon EX15 3DR

ROSEMARY SCHOOL OF NATURAL THERAPY
The Principal:
Rosemary Frances Lockyer
Cert Ed (Sci Biol: MBRA MIPTI ITEC IFR Accreditation)
● Anatomy ● Physiology & Massage
● Aromatherapy ● Reflexology
● Sports Therapy ● Nutrition/Diet
ITEC Examination, Diplomas
Small Groups, Individual attention
10 Pine Ridge, Newbury, Berkshire RG13 2NQ
Tel: (0635) 31679

From competence to excellence with... **NLP**
Find out how at our "FREE" monthly introductory evenings.
Tel: 071 794 0960
for Brochure and details

PPD
Pace Personal Development
86 South Hill Park,
London NW3 2SN
tel: 071 794 0960 Fax: 071 794 7366

The Sylvia Brearly School
– Harrogate and York –
ITEC Registered
Courses in Massage,
Aromatherpy and
Sports Injuries
Details: 0423 505707

The Raworth Centre
20-26 South Street, Dorking,
Surrey RH4 2HQ
Tel: 0306 742150

The Shiatsu College London,
Unit 62, 126-8 Barlby Road,
London W10
Tel: 081 964 1449

The Holistic School of Systems Therapy
Admin Office: 178 High Street,
Acton, London W3 9NN
Tel: 081 993 6351

The School of Homoeopathy
Yondercott House, Uffculme,
Devon EX15 3DR

Rosemary School of Natural Therapy
10 Pine Ridge, Newbury,
Berkshire RG13 2NQ
Tel: 0635 31679

Violet Hill Studios,
6 Violet Hill, St John's Wood,
London NW8 9EB
Telephone:
071 624 6101/081 458 5368

Midlands School of Massage
Nottingham
Tel: 0602 472263

Michael Mallows
Power², 37 Layfield Road
Hendon, London NW4 3UH

PPD Pace Personal Development
86 South Hill Park,
London NW3 2SN
Tel: 071 794 0960
Fax: 071 794 7366

Pellin Institute
15 Killyon Rd,
London SW8 2XS
Tel: 071 720 4499

The Bates Method (Vision Education)
The Bates Association of Great Britain
Friars Court,
11 Tarmount Lane
Shoreham-by-Sea
W Sussex BN43 6RQ

NATURAL HEALING CENTRE
Courses on Healing, Crystals,
Meditation, Aromatherapy
and Reflexology
For further details contact
Kathleen Huddlestone
72 Pasture Road, Goole, North Humberside DN14 6HE
Tel: 0405 769119

MIDLANDS SCHOOL OF MASSAGE
Call Nottingham
0602 472263

The National Association of Counsellors,
Hypnotherapists and Psychotherapists
offers a comprehensive training course leading to its Diploma
in Counselling Skills, Hypnotherapy and Psychotherapy.
*For full details and dates of next courses, please contact
the Director of Studies Anne Billings*
145 Coleridge Road, Cambridge CB1 3PN
enclosing 2 x 2nd class stamps for a prospectus

Pellin

Three-year part-time training course in Gestalt Psychotherapy and Counselling for women and men.
Courses begin January and October
Intensive Therapy Holidays in Agripoli, Southern Italy
July to September

**PELLIN INSTITUTE
15 Killyon Road
London SW8 2XS
Telephone 071-720 4499**

HYPNOSIS

Train for private practice with Europe's largest group of Hypnotherapists, the international association of Hypno-analysts. Top UK diploma course since 1981
Choose distance learning or group training
Phone for **FREE** prospectus and demo cassette
(Nationwide Register of Practitioners Included)

**HYPNOTHERAPY CONTROL BOARD
PO BOX 180,
BOURNEMOUTH BH3 7YR**
Telephone
0202 311191 (24 hrs)

RAWORTH CENTRE
COLLEGE FOR SPORTS THERAPY & NATURAL MEDICINE

TRAINING IN NATURAL MEDICINE AND SPORTS THERAPY

Train for a new career as a therapist or acquaint yourself with the many therapies gaining new respect and credibility in the Nineties.
Fully accredited Diploma courses full and part time, weekend study, special summer school programmes and introductory seminars.

- NATURAL HEALTH PRACTITIONERS DIPLOMA
- MASTERS DIPLOMA IN SPORTS THERAPY
- DIPLOMA IN HOLISTIC AROMATHERAPY
- NUTRITION CONSULTANTS DIPLOMA
- REFLEXOLOGY PRACTITIONERS DIPLOMA
- SWEDISH, HOLISTIC, THERAPEUTIC & SPORTS MASSAGE
- ACUPRESSURE & APPLIED KINESOLOGY

Over 2500 therapists trained since 1983
Prospectus The Raworth Centre
20-26 South Street, Dorking, Surrey RH4 2HQ
Tel: 0306 742150

Professional training in
Shiatsu and Oriental Medicine
with
The Shiatsu College

3 year weekend or weekday courses at our venue in London W10

- Regular introductory weekends
- Student clinic
- Post Graduate courses

For our new 1994 prospectus & booking information please send 4 x 1st class stamps to:

**The Shiatsu College London, Unit 62, 126-8 Barlby Road, London W10
Tel: 081 964 1449**

The School of Physical Therapies Group
ITEC Registered Schools

ITEC Courses
Therapeutic Massage,
Aromatherapy, Reflexology,
Sports Therapy & Nutrition

Other Courses
Touch for health, Dowsing & Radionic Homoeopathy
and many other Post Graduate Courses

All Schools have practicing therapists

For details phone your local school:
**Basingstike 0256 475728
Kingston 081 546 0290**

The *S.E.E.D* Institute
10, Magnolia Way, Fleet
Hants GU13 9JZ
Tel/Fax: 0252 626448

Committed to Health & Vitality

TSI offers the following two-day, post Graduate Courses:

In association with Shirley Price Aromatherapy

* Aromatherapy & Learning Disabilities
* Aromatherapy & Public Speaking
* Aromatherapy AIDS & HIV
* Remedial/Sport-Injury Massage
* Aromatherapy & Ayurveda
* Aromatherapy & Children

PLUS **Specialised two-day Courses**

* Introduction to Aromatherapy
* Aromatherapy & Children
* Aromatherapy & Learning Disabilities
* Nutrition -(1-3)
* Advanced Remedial Massage
* Iridology -(1-3)
* Balanced Health (Kinesiology)
* Essence of Counselling
* Business Administration Workshop

Locations: **Hants, Northants, Herts, Leics, Scotland**
(others considered for 10+ participants)
Apply sae (large A4) to Courses Secretary, Ref 'A&C'

SELF EXPLORATION EDUCATION DEVELOPMENT

Michael Mallows
creates
Power²

Workshops and Tapes.
London, Essex, Shropshire

The Power to...
Let go of Guilt
Empower Relationships
Love the Child Within
Write Creatively
& more.
Large SAE for details to
Power²
37 Layfield Road
Hendon, London NW4 3UH

BRETFORTON HALL CLINIC

STUDENTS ACCEPTED FOR TRAINING IN CYMATIC THERAPY ARE ELIGIBLE FOR CAREER DEVELOPMENT LOANS.
ALL STUDENTS HAVING PASSED AND QUALIFIED ARE ALSO ELIGIBLE FOR AN INTERNATIONAL UNIVERSITY DEGREE
ASK OR WRITE FOR DETAILS TO:

SECRETARY, BRETFORTON HALL SCIENTIFIC AND NATUROPATHIC MEDICAL TRAINING ESTABLISHMENT
VALE OF EVESHAM, WORCESTER WR 11 5JH
TEL: 0386 830537

MSM

Manchester School of Massage

INTRODUCTORY & DIPLOMA COURSES

MASSAGE AROMATHERAPY REFLEXOLOGY SPORTS THERAPY ONSITE-MASSAGE SHIATSU

77 RUSSELL ROAD, MANCHESTER, M16 8AR

TEL: 061 862 9752

The UK Training College
For Complementary Health
Care Studies
Exmoor Street,
London W10 6DZ
Tel: 081 964 1206

Solaire College of Natural
Therapies
ITEC Registered School
Personalised professional
tuituion in all subjects.
Lucas Close, Yateley,
Camberley, Surrey GU17 7JD
Tel: 0252 873334

Hypnotherapy Control Board
PO Box 180, Bournemouth
BH3 7YR
Tel: 0202 311191 (24 hrs)

Therapy Training College
8&10 Balaclava Road, Kings
Heath, Birmingham B14 7SG
Tel: 021 444 5435

The National College of
Hypnosis and Psychotherapy
12 Cross Street,
Nelson, Lancs BB9 7EN
Tel: 0282 699378
Fax: 0282 698633

The Pearl Healing Centre
37 Carew Road, Thornton
Heath, Surrey CR7 7RF
Tel: 081 689 1771

Bretforton Hall Scientific and
Naturopathic Medical Training
Establishment
Vale of Evesham,
Worcester WR11 5JH
Tel: 0386 830537

Manchester School of
Massage
77 Russell Road, Manchester
M16 8AR
Tel: 061 862 9752

British School of Reflexology
92 Sheering Road, Old Harlow
Essex
Tel: 0279 429060

The Institute of Traditional
Herbal Medicine and
Aromatherapy
15 Coolhurst Road,
London N8 8EP
Tel: 081 348 3755

Cheshire School of Natural
Therapies
129 Orford Lane, Warrington
WA2 7AR
Tel: 0244 301246

The Gerda Boyesen Centre
Acacia House, Centre Avenue,
Acton Park, London W3 7JX
Tel: 081 746 0499

Athena Counselling Services

FREEPOST (BR614) BRIGHTON BN2 2ZZ
TELEPHONE: (0273) 697376 - FAX: (0273) 670181

Sometimes life is not easy at all. We can help you with the following:
1. THERAPIES
2. COUNSELLING
3. HEALING
4. PSYCHOMETRICS
5. WORKSHOPS
6. TAPES
7. BOOKS
8. WORKSHOP TAPE SETS

(Wholesale discounts on items 6-8)
For full information on any of our products reply free by returning the coupon below
Please send me your full list of the products ticked below

| 1 | 2 | 3 | 4 | 5 | 6 | 7 | 8 |

Please print in capitals
Title: MS/MISS/MRS/MR _____ initials _____
Name _____
Address _____
_____
Postcode _____
Phone _____

Hypnotherapy Training
under the auspices of the Association of Qualified Curative Hypnotherapists. Practical weekend courses commence each spring and autumn for those who successfully pass the 3-month home-study section. Full details write or phone:
Therapy Training College 8&10 Balaclava Road, Kings Heath, Birmingham B14 7SG Tel: 021 444 5435

Violet Hill Studios
Centre for Healing and Creative Arts
A beutifully restored 18th century barn with an extensive selection of therapies, workshops and art exhibition
6 Violet Hill, St John's Wood, London NW8 9EB
Tel: 071 624 6101/081 458 5368

THE PEARL HEALING CENTRE
Crystal and Colour Courses PHC
Sounds and Palmistry.
Metamorphic Technique Hypnotherapy
Healing by appointment
Crystals, Gemstones, Books by mail order
37 Carew Road, Thornton Heath, Surrey CR7 7RF
Telephone 081 689 1771

The British School of Reflexology

PRINCIPAL Ann Gillanders MBSR,MBSA

TRAIN TO BE A REFLEXOLOGY PRACTITIONER THROUGH THE MOST PROFESSIONAL ORGANISATION.

ANN GILLANDERS HAS BEEN INVOLVED IN TEACHING, PRACTISING AND PROMOTING REFLEXOLOGY INTERNATIONALLY FOR 17 YEARS AND HAS A WEALTH OF KNOWLEDGE TO IMPART

THE SCHOOL HAS EXPANDED VENUES NOW TO INCLUDE

LONDON HARLOW NOTTINGHAM HARROGATE BRISTOL

OUR FOUR PART TRAINING COURSES ARE COMBINED WITH CORRESPONDENCE STUDY. THE COURSE PREPARES PRACTITIONERS FOR ENTRY INTO THE BRITISH REGISTER NOW FORMED

A LIST OF REGISTERED REFLEXOLOGISTS IN YOUR AREA MAY BE OBTAINED BY SENDING A SAE(9X5)

FOR DETAILS OF TRAINING SEND A 40P STAMP FOR A FULL BROCHURE TO:

**BRITISH SCHOOL OF REFLEXOLOGY
92 SHEERING ROAD,
OLD HARLOW, ESSEX
TEL 0279 429060**

Institute of Traditional Herbal Medicine and Aromatherapy
(est 1980)

AROMATHERAPY MASSAGE DIPLOMA COURSE

16-weekend professional qualification courses:
50 essential oils, Massage, Oriental Diagnosis, Cranial Therapy, Anatomy and Physiology

Write: ITHMA, 15 Coolhurst Road, London N8 8EP Tel: 081 348 3755

THE COMPLEMENTARY HEALTH PRACTICE

Natural healing in conjunction with complementary and orthodox therapies provides a truly holistic approach to good health.
Treatments include manipulation, acupuncture, massage (remedial and aromatherapy), hypnotherapy, reflexology, allergy testing, homoeopathy, herbalism.

For more details and appointments telephone:
Newcastle-under-Lyme 0782 712127
Harley Street 071 636 6540

THE UK TRAINING COLLEGE
For Complementary Health Care Studies

Exmoor Street, London W10 6DZ
Tel: 081 964 1206
Daytime and Weekend Programmes include:
A BTEC Continuing Education Certificate in Complementary Health Care
&
The Joint Skills Testing Certificate of the City & Guilds and The UK Training College –
Hypnotherapy and Counselling
(Foundation Level)

Prospectus from:
The Administrator,
UK Training College, Exmoor Street,
London W10 6DZ
(Large SAE 41p)

**THE GERDA BOYESEN CENTRE
BIODYNAMIC PSYCHOLOGY AND MASSAGE**

A natural approach to deep relaxation. Individual treatments by graduate therapists. Complete training courses. Short courses.

Acacia House, Centre Avenue, Acton Park,
London W3 7JX Tel: 081 746 0499

WARRINGTON ✦ CHESHIRE

INTERNATIONALLY RECOGNISED CERTIFICATES AND DIPLOMAS IN

**MASSAGE ANATOMY – PHYSIOLOGY
– AROMATHERAPY – REFLEXOLOGY –
SPORTS INJURIES**

CHESHIRE SCHOOL OF NATURAL THERAPIES
129 ORFORD LANE, WARRINGTON, WA2 7AR
TEL: 0244 301246 (ITEC REGISTERED SCHOOL)
ACCOMODATION AVAILABLE

School of Massage

The Bates Method - *vision education*
for information on
● teachers ● training courses ● workshops ● publications

write enclosing a 9x6 sae to: The Bates Association of Great Britain, Friars Court, 11 Tarmount Lane, Shoreham-by-Sea BN43 6RQ

HEALTH CENTRES & CLINICS

Dr Paul Scarrow
B Med Sci BM BS
Medi Scene Health Care
See ad under Biofeedback,
Healthy Living and Well
Being and Muscle Learning
Therapy Tel/Fax: 0777 708060

Natural Health Clinic,
286 Preston Road, Harrow,
Middx HA3 0QA
Tel 081-908 4272

The Bridge Street Clinic
11 Bridge Street, Winchester
Established over 20 years in the practice of
Natural medicine
Osteopathy, Medical Herbalism, Homoeopathy
Tel: 0962 853260

The Gerda Boyesen Centre
Biodynamic Psychology and Massage
Acacia House, Centre Avenue,
Acton Park, London W3 7JX
Tel: 081 746 0499

Acu Medic Centre
101-103 Camden High Street,
London NW1 7JN
Tel: 071 388 5783/388 6704
Fax: 071 387 5766
Telex: 269460 ACUMED G

Kay McCarroll DHP MC MIPC
The Hendon Practice
12 Golders Rise
London NW4
Tel: 081 202 9747

Rex Thurstan DMO M PhyA MBEOA
The Cottage Clinic,
25 Sea Road, Bexhill-on-Sea, Sussex
Tel: 0424 222070

Flint House
Natural Health Clinic and Learning Centre
41 High Street, Lewes, Sussex
(entrance in St Nicholas Lane)
Tel: 0273 473388

Complementary Medicine Centre, 9 Corporation Street, Taunton, Somerset TA1 4AJ
Tel: 0823 325022

FLINT HOUSE
Natural Health Clinic and Learning Centre
Daily tratments in a wide range of natural therapies.
Weekend workshops run by inspring leaders.
Beneficial day and evening courses.
We would welcome a visit at
41 High Street Lewes (entrance in St Nicholas Lane)
or please **Telephone: 0273 473388**

THE COTTAGE CLINIC
REX THURSTAN DMO M PhyA MBEOA
OSTEOPATHY ● PHYSIOTHERAPY
SOFT LASER LIGHT THERAPY
25 Sea Road, Bexhill-on-Sea, Sussex TN40 1EE

The Heyokah Centre
FOR HEALING ARTS & CRAFTS

Books, crystals, oils, candles,
native American crafts

wide range of healing therapies
Tai Chi, Chi Kung, Reiki, Counselling Floatation Room

Visit us for lunch

2 Humphrey Street, Swansea
Tel: 0792 457880

Kay McCarroll DHP MC MIPC
Kinesiology Instructor ✦ Therapist for TFH
Dyslexia
Sports and Stress Problems
The Hendon Practice
12 Golders Rise London NW4
Tel: 081 202 9747

COMPLEMENTARY MEDICINE SERVICES
(incorporating the Allergy Centre)
9 CORPORATION STREET, TAUNTON, SOMERSET TA1 4AJ
Tel: 0823 325022

Do you need help with recurrent health problems?
For example Candida (thrush), Cystitis, Irritable Bowel, Allergies, Fluid Retention, Hyperactivity (children), Stress, Migraine, Pre-menstral Syndrome etc.
Come and talk to us we are right next to the library
Our practitioners are fully qualified and they are always happy to spend 10 minutes discussing a particular problem with you prior to making an appointment

● Acupuncture ● Aromotherapy ● Chiropodists
● Allergy therapy ● Food allergy testing ● Herbal medicine
● Holistic massage ● Hypnotherapy ● Homoeopathy
● Iridology ● Osteopathy ● Psychotherapy ● Reflexology
● Shiatsu ● Vitamin & mineral deficiency testing

Natural Choice Therapy
Ce'ntre
24 St John Street, Ashbourne,
Derbyshire DE6 1GH
Tel: 0335 346096S

Natural Healing Centre
72 Pasture Road, Goole,
North Humberside DN14 6HE
Tel: 0405 769119.

HEALTH RETREATS AND HOLIDAYS

PRODUCTS AND SERVICES

Centre for Creative Healing,
6 Violet Hill,
St John's Wood,
London NW8 9EB
tel: 071 624 6101

The Nutri Centre
7 Park Crescent
London W1N 3HE
Tel: 071 436 5122
Fax: 071 436 5171

Primrose Healing Centre,
9 St George's Mews,
London NW1 8XE
Tel: 071 5r86 0148

Complementary Health Clinic
65 Grosvenor Road,
Tunbridge Wells, Kent
Tel: 0892 518999
Fax: 0892 540834

The Complementary Health
Practice
Newcastle-under-Lyme
Tel: 0782 7123127
Harley Street
Tel: 071 636 6540

The Trinity Centre,
21 Trinity Street, Colchester,
Essex.
Tel: 0206 823723

DEVON
Yeo Cottage
Breaks for Peace,
Relaxation, Healing, Spiritual
Counselling and your
Thatched Cottage,
2 miles Totnes. Michael Cox,
Yeo Cottage, Sandwell Lane,
Totnes, Devon
Tel: 0803 868157

FAR WEST CORNWALL
Homely wholefood
vegetarian B&B in old
Cornish cottage close to
beautiful rugged coast,
sandy beaches, ancient
sites. Contact Richard and
Dr Annie Hatfield who also
practice healing, counselling
and acupuncture.
Tel: St Buryan 0736 810723

GWENT
Real Lighthouse on
crossing leylines
Built 1821, Grade II listed.
Superb B&B accommoda-
tion, floatation tank &
W Reich's orgone
accummulator.
Other therapies available.
Peaceful, off the beaten
track and different
Tel: 0633 810126/815860

Biosun UK Ltd
Sheepcoates Lane
Great Totham, Maldon,
Essex CM9 8NT
Tel: 0621 788411

Surrey Yoga Centre
Church Farm House,
Spring Close Lane, Cheam,
Surrey SM3 8PU
Yoga products, practice
cassettes
Tel: 081 644 0309

Wholistic Research
Company
Dept CH, Bright Haven,
Robin's Lane
Lolworth, Cambridge
CB3 8HH
Tel: 0954 781074

Neti Pots for salt water nasal
cleaning. Hand-thrown ash
glaze stoneware £6.50 plus
£2 p&p.
Joan Smith
Stream Cottage,
21 Downview Avenue,
Ferring, West Sussex
BN12 6QN

The Pearl Healing Centre
Crystals, Gemstones, Books
by mail order
37 Carew Road, Thornton
Heath, Surrey CR7 7RF
Tel: 081 689 1771

The Heyokah Centre
FOR HEALING ARTS & CRAFTS

Books, crystals, oils, candles, native American crafts

wide range of healing therapies
Tai Chi, Chi Kung, Reiki, Counselling Floatation Room

Visit us for lunch
2 Humphrey Street, Swansea
Tel: 0792 457880

CELESTIAL DESIGNS

Aromatherapy
100% pure essential oils.
Oil vaporizers. Books.
Charts and ALL your
Aromatherapy Needs
Alternative Workshops and
Residential Courses.

For all enquiries and further information please contact:
Celestial Designs Aromatherapy
Tan-y-Gyrt Hall, Nantglyn, Nr Denbigh, Clwyd LL16 5DP
Tel: 0745 70411/70308

EAR CANDLES
BUAV APPROVED PRODUCTS

- **HOPI INDIAN REMEDY** used for sinusitis, tinnitus, headaches and stress and most ENT problems
- **CELL ENERGY CREAMS** an edible all natural product for skin disorders, cellulite, strains, tensions, rejuvenates and softens skin
- **HIGH ENERGY PIEZO** electric therapy system, no batteries or mains, used for needle-less acupuncture, physiotherapy, rheumatism, arthritis, sports injuries. 14 day free trial.
- **DEODORANT STONES** economical, natural crystal deodorant

BIOSUN UK Ltd
Tel: 0621 788411

Sheepcoates Lane, Great Totham, Maldon, Essex CM9 8NT

GENUINE S C SPIRITUAL

A real and personal; answer to
ANY PROBLEM
Just send £10 stating need for
PERSONALLY PROGRAMMED CRYSTAL
in velvet pouch to :
Spiritual Crystals, 3 Rhiwbank Avenue, Colwyn Bay LL29 7PH Tel: (0492) 531250

Acu Medic Centre

Offers a wide range of books on acupuncture and natural medicine for professionals and the general public and a comprehensive selection of acupuncture equipment. Chinese herbs and nutritional products

101-103 Camden High Street, London NW1 7JN
Tel: 071 388 5783/388 6704 Fax: 071 387 5766
Telex: 269460 ACUMED G

RELAXATION & SELF-HEALING
WITH KATE WILLIAMS

Meditative exercises to relax, revitalise and ground you

Follow Kate's voice to gently unwind and find a source of energy and peace within. £7.50 inc p&p.
For full details and order form
RING 081 8887927

GEOGRAPHICAL INDEX

Only a small number of the many therapists working in alternative medicine are listed under each individual therapy, but a contact address for a governing body or national organiser or training school is given. This index lists therapists by county and show what treatments are they can offer. Full addresses are given under the relevant therapy headings. A number of alternative health centres ofering a wide range of therapies are listed on pages 75 and 76 and schools and centres running courses for those who want to take their knowledge of complementary medicine further can be found on pages 69 to 74.

KEY

Ac –	Acupuncture	Dm –	Dance Movement Therapy	Nlp –	Neuro Linguistic Programming
All –	Allergy Therapy	Dt –	Dietary Therapeutics		
Am –	Anthroposophical Medicine	Fm –	Feldenkrais Method	Nt –	Nutritional therapy
Ap –	Acupressure	Ft –	Floatation Therapy	O –	Osteopathy
Ar –	Aromatherapy	H –	Healing	Ot –	Ozone Therapy
Art –	Art Therapy	Hm –	Herbal Medicine	Pc –	Psychic Counselling
At –	Alexander Technique	Ho –	Homoeopathy	Ps –	Psychotherapy
Ast	Aston Patterning	Hw –	Hellerwork	Pt –	Polarity Therapy
Au –	Autogenic Training	Hy –	Hypnotherapy	Rb –	Rebirthing
Bf –	Biofeedback			Rg –	Regression Therapy
Bm –	Bates Method	Ip –	Integral Psychoanalysis	Rk –	Reiki
Cg –	Counselling	Ir –	Iridology	Ro –	Rolfing
Cgt –	Crystal Healing/Gem Therapy	Ki –	Kinesiology	Rt –	Radiance Technique
		M –	Massage	Rx –	Reflexology
Ch –	Colonic Hydrotherapy	Me –	Meditation	Sh –	Shamanism
Cm –	Chinese Medicine	Ms –	Mesotherapy	Ss –	Stress Management
Co –	Colour Therapy	Msv –	Music, Sound and Voice Therapies	Su –	Shiatsu
Cp –	Chiropractic			Tr –	Tape Relaxation
Cst –	Craniosacral Therapy	Mt –	Megavitamin Therapy	Y –	Yoga
Ct –	Chelation Therapy	Nb –	Natural Beauty		

AVON	Amphora Aromatics	Ar
	Anna Orren	Ro
	Bath Natural Health Clinic	Bm
	John Seymour Associates	Nlp
BEDS	Michael Boyce	Ki
	Sarah Wale	Su
	Yoga for Health Foundation	Y
BERKS	Jean Taylor	Cg, Me
	Jill Norfolk	Ar
	Mrs Naomi Shepherd	Rx
	Natural Therapy Centre	Rx
	Tamara Burnet-Smith	Au
BUCKS	Dr Alice Green	Au
	Jacob Briskham	Hm
CHESHIRE	Mrs Jones	Ar,Hy,M,Rx
	Natural Therapy Centre	Ar
	Springfield Clinic of Natural Healing	H,Hm,Ps
	The Aroma Therapy Shop	Ar
CUMBRIA	Salon Elysee Hair and Beauty	Rx
DERBYSHIRE	Natural Choice Therapy Centre	Ac,At,Ar,Cp,Hm,Ho,Ip,Ir,M, Mm,Ps,Rx,Su
DEVON	Kobashi	Ar
	Rita Benor	Au
	The Devon School of Shiatsu	Su
	The Institute of Crystal and Gem Therapists	Cgt
DORSET	Derek Law	O
	Galen Homoeopathics	Ho
	Josephine Pridmore	Su
ESSEX	British School of Reflexology	Rx
	Essex School of Massage	M
	International Academy of Holistic Studies	Ar
	Meg Reid	Rx,Rk
	Mrs Dawson	Hy,M,Rx
	Ms G Leddy	Hm
	Nature Care School of Massage	M
	Rosemary Cunningham	Ki,M
	Rosemary Ryan	Rx
	Sharon Jarvis	Sd
	Stuart Wetherell	Hy
GLOUCESTERSHIRE	Alice Friend	H
	Cheltenham Hoths School of Reflexology	Rx
	Philippa Hunter	Ar
	The Dug Out	Cgt
GREATER MANCHESTER	Manchester School of Massage	Ar,M,Rx

HAMPSHIRE	Allergy Relief Products	All
	Elizabeth Lewin	Au
	Mahmood Chaudry	Ho
	New Horizon Aromatics	Ar,M
	Sheila Parry	At,Bm
	The SEED Institute	Ar,Ki,M,Me,Ps,Ss
HERTS	Dr Elisabeth Dancey	Ct,Me
	Jane Bird	Au
	Janet Love	H
	Margaret Montgomery	Bm
	Roger Golten	Hw
HUMBERSIDE	Natural Healing Centre	Ar,H,Ho,Hy,Ir,M
KENT	British School of Shiatsu-Do (Maidstone)	Dt,Su
	Complementary Health Clinic	Ft
	Liongate Clinic	Ct,Ot
	Magda Williams	Dm
	Mrs Shirley Crawford	At
	Susan Fairley	Ch,Co
LANCASHIRE	Complex Homoeopathy (Bolton) Ltd	Ho
	National College of Hypnosis and Psychotherapy	Hy,Ps
LEICESTERSHIRE	Shirley Price Aromatherapy College	Ar
	Terry Larder	Ki,Rx
LONDON	Acu-medic Centre	Ac,Ar,Cm
	Ainsworths Homoeopathic Pharmacy	Ho
	Anthony Attenborough	Bm
	Bloomsbury Alexander Centre	At
	Brenda Coverdale	Ar
	Centre for Creative Healing	At,Co,Cst,H,Ho,Ki,Rk
	Centre of Integral Psychoansalysis	Ip
	Chandra Vashisht	Bm
	David Glassman	At,Bm
	Dr Alice Greene	Au,Ho
	Dr Marsh	Ar
	Eagle's Wing Centre for Contemporary Shamanism	Sh
	Fleur	Ar
	Fook Song Acupuncture & Chinese Herbal Practitioners Training Coll	Ac,Cm
	Heather Algar	Ac
	Ingrid St Clare	Ast,Me,Msv
	Institute for Optimum Nutrition	Nt
	Institute of Traditional Herbal Medicine and Aromatherapy	Ar,Hm
	Jenni Crewdson	Ro